FIELD&
STREAM'S
Guide to the Outdoors

FIELD & STREAM'S
GUIDE TO
OUTDOOR
SURVIVAL

T. EDWARD NICKENS
AND THE EDITORS OF FIELD & STREAM

Gareth Stevens
PUBLISHING

FIELD&
STREAM'S
Guide to the Outdoors

FIELD & STREAM'S
GUIDE TO
OUTDOOR
SURVIVAL

T. EDWARD NICKENS
AND THE EDITORS OF *FIELD & STREAM*

 Gareth Stevens
PUBLISHING

CONTENTS

*"Difficulties are just things
to overcome, after all."*

—Ernest Shackleton

The Skin of Your Teeth

Now you've gone and done it. Gone too far or gone overboard. Lost your way, left your flashlight at camp, let darkness catch you in the woods without a single match. At the moment, it doesn't matter how you got here. What matters is that it's all up to you, bud. Live or die.

These days, it's all too easy to think that survival skills are a lost and useless art—techniques as practical as, say, knowing how to plow with an ox. The reality, however, is that modern life has figured out new ways to put the unprepared in precarious situations. For starters, it's easier than ever to gain access to remote, rugged country. Thanks to floatplanes, helicopters, even frequent-flyer miles, more and more of us are going farther and farther into the wilds. When we get there, we rely too heavily on things that go blank when the batteries die. And perversely, just when we really need to know how to signal with smoke or build a fire in the rain, the skills necessary to dig our way out of the hole have all but eroded away.

Only once have I come close to dying in the outdoors. Pinned underwater in a remote Alaska river, I clawed to the surface to face days filled with fear as my party portaged canoes through wilderness forest so thick we often couldn't see 10 feet into the woods. We swapped turns as point man, burrowing through the brush with a shotgun in one hand and bear spray in the other.

But I have to wonder: How often do truly skillful hunters and anglers skirt disaster—without even knowing it—because they know how to stay *out* of trouble? If you're smart enough to carry three ways to start a fire in your pack or pockets, you negate the necessity of a fire plough. Know how to find your way by deliberate offset, and you might not ever have to descend a cliff on a single rope.

The wolves have howled at my door only a time or two, but there have been plenty of instances when I was glad that I knew how to coax fire from damp

wood, because it made life easier when I finally made it back to camp. I'm glad I know how to take a back bearing and navigate by map and compass because those skills mean I can plumb big woods with the confidence that I will be able to find my way back to the truck. The fact that I can run a whitewater rapid—or swim it safely if it turns out I'm not quite the paddler that I had imagined—has opened up worlds of wilderness walleye and salmon and smallmouth bass.

Truth be told, having a few good survival skills is just as likely to come in handy when you need to whip up a quick, hot trail lunch as it is when you need to warm your frozen fingers enough to weave a brush raft that you will use to cross the swollen river before the raging wildfire burns you alive. Much of the value of knowing how to survive when you lose all your chips is that the knowledge helps you play a better hand when you're still holding a few decent cards.

And let's be honest: The ability to craft a back-country deathstar or use hot coals to hollow out a river cane blowgun—you're just plain cooler for having those aces up your sleeve.

So the next time some city slicker chuckles at the dryer lint you're saving for a DIY fire starter, just remind yourself: You may never need this stuff—until suddenly, critically, you do. Until you wander too far into the woods. Lose your way. Break down, fall down, or go down the wrong trail. Until you have to survive, for an hour or a long, cold night, or longer. Then you'll be happy you know how to survive. Lucky is the man who can spark flame and sleep soundly on a fire bed, a smile on his face, ready for the long hike home in the morning.
—*T. Edward Nickens*

1 CREATE SMOKE IN THE MIDDLE OF THE OCEAN

Lose your motor miles from shore, and you'll need to attract attention in a big way. That means smoke on the water. Here's how to get noticed no matter where you are.

STEP 1 Grab a square throwable personal flotation device (PFD) or snap out a boat seat cushion. Tie a 10-foot line to one corner and tether the other end of the line to a downwind boat cleat.

STEP 2 Find something made of rubber that will hold a bit of fuel—a sneaker, dive fin, or foam drink insulator. Balance this item on the boat cushion or throwable PFD and siphon gas into it.

STEP 3 Light your signal fire and then use an oar or gaff to push it safely downwind from you. —T.E.N.

2 SURVIVE A FALL THROUGH THE ICE

Say "hard water" in northern regions, and folks know you're not complaining about rinsing soap out of your hair. In these cold climes, hard water is ice—as in ice fishing. And up here, you'd better know how to climb out when the water is not as hard as you thought. Here's a handy self-rescue device that has saved many a life.

HOW IT'S DONE Cut two 5-inch sections from a broomstick or 1-inch wooden dowel. On each of the pieces, drill a hole into one end that's slightly smaller than the diameter of whatever nails you have handy, and another hole crosswise at the other end. Drive a nail

into each end hole. Cut off the nailhead, leaving 1 inch of protruding nail. Sharpen with a file to a semi-sharp point. Thread a 6-foot length (or a length that's equal to your arm span) of parachute cord through the crosswise holes and tie off with stopper knots.

Thread one dowel through both coat sleeves. When you slip the coat on, keep the dowels just below your cuffs. If you do go through the ice, grab the dowels and drive the nails into the ice to drag yourself out. —T.E.N.

3 MAKE EMERGENCY MUKLUKS

Keep toes and feet intact with makeshift mukluks. Find some insulating material—a piece of fleece, sleeping pad, or boat carpet—and do the following for each foot.

STEP 1 Cut insulating material into a circle about 24 inches across.

STEP 2 Fold the circle of insulation into quarters.

STEP 3 Move one layer of the insulation aside and insert your foot into the folded material. There should be a single layer at the heel.

STEP 4 Alternate the remaining layers around your foot. Slip an outer shell—part of a tarp or even a pants leg cut from spare clothing—over the insulation.

STEP 5 Crisscross a piece of cord around the outer layer, or use duct tape to secure firmly. —T.E.N.

4 CALL FOR HELP IN ANY LANGUAGE

The international signal for distress is a sequence of short and long signals, designed for telegraph operators—three short, three long, three short. Adopted at the Berlin Radiotelegraphic Conference in 1906, the SOS sequence was based solely on its ease of transmitting. It does not mean "save our ship" or anything else you've heard. But you can transmit the code with just about any device imaginable: whistle blasts, car horns, gunshots, light flashes, even pots and pans. —T.E.N.

5 SURVIVE THE ROUGHEST NIGHT WITH A KNIFE

You can use a strong knife to turn a single conifer tree into an overnight bivvy. First, fell a 9-foot balsam or other evergreen and remove all the branches close to the trunk.

MAKE A BOUGH BED Cut the tips of the evergreen branches to 1 foot in length. Use wooden stakes to chock a 3-foot-long, 4-inch-diameter log (cut from the tree trunk) where you want the head of your bed to be. Shingle the boughs at a 45-degree angle pointing away from the foot of the bed. Compress tightly as you work your way down. Anchor with a second 3-foot-long log from the trunk chocked with wooden stakes.

GLEAN TINDER The low, dead branches and sucker twigs of conifers make excellent tinder. Carve a fuzz stick from the thickest branch. Gather wood shavings from the others by scraping with the knife held at a 90-degree angle to the twigs.

GIN POLE A FISH To cook a fish with no utensils, snip away all twigs from the longest branch. Sharpen the fat end and drive it into the ground at about a 45-degree angle. Chock it with a rock or Y-shaped stick. Run cord through a fish's mouth and gill like a stringer, tie it to the branch, and let it dangle and cook beside the fire. —T.E.N.

6 BUILD A FIRE IN THE RAIN

There are those who can and those who think they can. Here's how to be one of those who really can.

STEP 1 Allow three times as much time for fire building as you'd need in dry conditions. If you're hiking, gather dry tinder as you go along the trail.

STEP 2 Look down when looking for tinder. Dry tinder may be under rocks, ledges, and logs, and in tree hollows. The underside of leaning deadfalls can be dry in a downpour; chop out chunks of good wood. Conifer stumps hold flammable resins.

STEP 3 Look up. Search for dry kindling and fuel off the wet ground. Fallen branches that are suspended in smaller trees will likely be rot-free. Locate a dense conifer and harvest the low, dead twigs and branches that die off as the tree grows. Shred the bark with your fingers.

STEP 4 Make what you can't find. Use a knife or hatchet blade to scrape away wet wood surfaces.

As the fire sustains itself (a), construct a crosshatched "log cabin" of wet wood around it (b) with a double-layered roof (c). The top layer of wood will deflect rain while the lower level dries. —T.E.N.

a b c

7 RESET A DISLOCATED SHOULDER

You wrench your arm out of its socket while taking a nasty fall, or your buddy screams in pain while hoisting a deer into the truck. If you're far from a hospital, try this method for resetting a dislocated shoulder in the backcountry.

STEP 1 Create a weight of approximately 7 to 10 pounds with a rock or stuff sack full of sand or pebbles.

STEP 2 Have the victim lie face down on a rock, large log, or upside-down boat and get as comfortable as possible. Drape the affected arm over the makeshift gurney's edge so it hangs free at a 90-degree angle. Tie the weight to the wrist of the affected shoulder, being careful not to cut off blood circulation. As the weight pulls on the arm, muscles will relax and the shoulder will relocate. This could take 30 minutes. —T.E.N.

9 BOIL WATER FOR SAFE DRINKING

Without chemicals or a filtering or purifying device, the only option for disinfecting water is to bring it to a boil. But how long to simmer plain ol' H_2O? Heat will kill bacteria, viruses, and parasites before the water reaches 212 degrees F, so once the liquid is roiling—and has cooled down a bit—it's safe to drink.

But there's more to the process than simply setting a pot on a fire or stove. First, bring a small amount of water to a rapid boil, swirl it around the pot to clean the sides, and pour it out. Refill the pot and bring the fresh batch to a roiling boil. Pour a quarter-cup on the ground to help sterilize the rim of the container and then fill water bottles as needed. And be sure you don't pour disinfected water back into the water bottle you used to dip the dirty stuff from the creek in the first place.

Boiling water removes much of its oxygen and gives it a flat taste, so add a drink flavoring agent or pour the water back and forth between two clean containers to aerate it as it cools. —T.E.N.

8 MAKE A TINDER BUNDLE

Fire making does not end with the birth of a red-hot coal, nor does a glowing char cloth ensure that you're going to get a flame. You must transfer the coal or char cloth to a bundle of fine tinder before blowing it into flame. Good sources include dried grasses; lichens (including old man's beard); shavings from the inner bark of aspen, poplar, and cottonwood trees (which burn even when wet); and windblown seed or fluff. The tinder bundle should be roughly the size of a softball and loosely formed to allow air circulation.

To blow the bundle into a flame, make a small pocket in the center. Tuck the glowing coal or char cloth into the pocket and then loosely fold the edges around it. Next, pick up the bundle and gently blow on it. Once it has burst into flame, place it under a tepee formation of small twigs and add larger pieces until you establish a strong fire. —K.M.

10 SPEAR FISH IN A FUNNEL TRAP

Make the walls of the funnel trap with piled-up stones or tightly spaced sticks driven solidly into the river or lakebed. Once fish are in the trap, close the entrance, roil the water, and either spear them or net them with a seine made by tying a shirt or other cloth between two stout poles. —K.M.

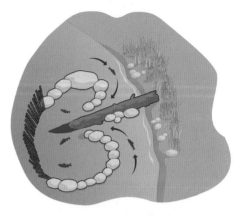

11 ASSESS YOUR SITUATION

It's decision time: Do you stay or go? If you're stuck at a campsite or next to a failed vehicle, you can wait until help arrives—or you can try hiking back to civilization. Assuming you're healthy, here's your checklist for deciding whether to sit tight or get going.

STAY IF:

☐ The campsite or vehicle is intact. It's a ready-made shelter—leave it only as a last resort.

☐ Your camp or vehicle has ample food and water.

☐ You need to conserve energy because you lack supplies or are injured.

☐ The site or vehicle is visible to searchers.

HIKE OUT IF:

☐ You're certain nobody is looking for you.

☐ You're sure of which way to go and how long it will take to reach help.

☐ You've got a well-stocked wilderness survival kit that you can carry. If you don't, you shouldn't be in the wilderness in the first place, should you? —R.J.

12 DRINK SNOW

Snacking on snow is fine until you're in a survival situation, when stuffing your face full of snow will consume critical energy reserves. To convert water from a frozen to a liquid state, choose ice over snow if possible, for it often contains fewer foreign objects that can carry pathogens, and ice will convert to more water than an equal volume of snow. Here are three ways to fill your water bottle from the hard stuff.

WATER MACHINE To melt snow or ice, snip a pea-size hole in the bottom corner of a T-shirt, pillowcase, or other makeshift fabric bag. Pack the bag with snow and hang it near a fire. Place a container under the hole to catch water melted by radiant heat. To keep the fabric from burning, refill the bag as the snow or ice melts.

FLAME ON Avoid scorching the pot—which will give the water a burned taste—by heating a small amount of "starter water" before adding snow or ice. Place the pot over a low flame or just a few coals and agitate frequently.

BODY HEAT You may have no other option than to use body heat to melt the snow. If so, put small quantities of snow or ice in a waterproof container and then place the container between layers of clothing next to your body—but not against your skin. A soft plastic bag works better than a hard-shell canteen. Shake the container often to speed up the process. —T.E.N.

13 CARRY 50 FEET OF ROPE ON YOUR FEET

Real parachute cord is rated to 550 pounds. It's made of a tough outer sheath rated to 200 pounds, which protects seven interior strands, each rated to 50 pounds. Take apart a single 3-foot length of paracord, and you'll have almost 25 feet of cordage. Use it to rig shelters and snares, lash knife blades to spears, fix broken tent poles—you name it. If you replace both laces with paracord as soon as you buy a new pair of boots, you'll never be without a stash. Just make sure you buy the 550-pound-test cord. —T.E.N.

14 AIM A MAKESHIFT SIGNAL MIRROR

The best commercial signal mirrors are made with aiming devices. But there are ways to aim a jerry-rigged signal mirror—aluminum foil wrapped neatly around a playing card, or the shiny interior surface of an aluminum can—that can also attract attention.

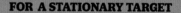

FOR A MOVING TARGET

STEP 1 Hold the mirror in one hand and extend the other in front, fingers spread to form a V between your fingers and thumb.

STEP 2 Move your hand until the target rests in the V.

STEP 3 Angle the mirror so the reflected sunlight flashes through the V and directly onto the target.

FOR A STATIONARY TARGET

STEP 1 Drive an aiming stake chest-high into the ground, or choose a similar object such as a broken sapling or rock.

STEP 2 Stand so the target, the top of the aiming stake, and the signal mirror are in a straight line.

STEP 3 Move the mirror so the reflected sunlight flashes from the top of the aiming stake to the target. —T.E.N.

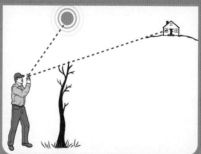

15 READ A BEAR'S MIND

A defensive bear (a) will appear stressed and unsure of how to act, pacing about and popping its jaws. Talk to it in a very calm voice. Don't throw anything. When it is not moving toward you, move away from it slowly and carefully. A stumble now could provoke a charge. If the bear continues to approach you, stop. Stand your ground and continue talking calmly. If the bear charges, use your spray or gun; wait until the last possible moment before hitting the dirt.

A predatory bear (b) isn't intent on rendering you harmless but rather on rendering you digestible. If a bear is aware of your presence and approaches in a nondefensive, unconcerned manner, get very serious. Speak to it in a loud, firm voice. Try to get out of the bear's direction of travel but do not run. If the animal follows, stop again and make a stand. Shout at the bear and stare at it. Make yourself appear larger—step up on a rock or move uphill. Prepare for a charge. —T.E.N.

16 HURL A BACK-COUNTRY DEATHSTAR

Boomerang, schmoomerang. When you need to kill a rabbit, grouse, or squirrel with a stick, throw a backcountry deathstar. Cut two pieces of straight, wrist-thick hardwood about 2 to 3 feet long. Carve a notch in the middle of each stick and lash them tightly together with notches together. Sharpen each of the four points. Throw it sidearm for a whirling, slashing disk of death—or, in a survival situation, life. —T.E.N.

17 EAT ROADKILL

If you make it to a road, rescue is likely just around the corner. If not, however, even the least-traveled highways can serve as a buffet for the feral forager. To separate plate-worthy roadkill from vulture food, follow these guidelines:

BODY CHECK Look for critters that have been clipped and tossed to the side of the road. If you have to use a flat shovel to retrieve your prize, well. . . .

SMELL TEST Any hunter knows what fresh dead meat smells like. Give the carcass a good sniff.

CLOUDY EYES Pass it up; it's been dead awhile.

FLEA CHECK If you find maggots, keep it out of your shopping cart. Fleas and ticks, however, are a good indicator of a fresh kill. —T.E.N.

18 SURVIVE A FALL OVERBOARD

More than 200 sportsmen drown or succumb to hypothermia in boating accidents each year; most deaths occur when the boat capsizes or the sportsman falls overboard. Statistically, no other hunting or fishing activity has a higher fatality rate. Here's how to protect yourself.

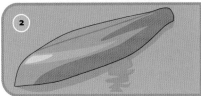

THE CAPISTRANO FLIP

Because cold water conducts heat from the body much more rapidly than air, it's vitally important that you get out of the water. Canoes and narrow-beam boats can often be righted by a maneuver called the Capistrano flip. Turn your boat completely over (1) and then duck into the pocket of air trapped beneath it (2). Hold the gunwales at the center of the boat. If there are two of you, face each other a couple of feet apart. Lift one edge slightly out of the water. Then scissor-kick, push to break the boat free of the surface, and flip it upright over that lifted edge (3). —K.M.

19 TAKE A BACK BEARING

The reading from a back bearing gives you a compass direction to follow to return to your starting position. More important, it can correct lateral drift off of your intended direction of travel, which is what occurs each time an obstacle forces you to move off your intended line. Once you have your forward bearing, turn around 180 degrees and take a back bearing. (Say you're moving in a direction of travel of 45 degrees, or northeast. Your back bearing would be 225 degrees.)

As you move toward your destination, occasionally turn around and point the direction of travel arrow on your compass back to your last location. The white end of the compass needle should point there. If not, regain the correct line by moving until the needle lines up. —T.E.N.

20 DEATH TRAP

Greenhill Rapids is a 3/4-mile-long cauldron across the backbone of an esker, one of those weird rock formations created by the dragging fingers of a receding glacier. There's a dogleg turn in the middle and canoe-swamping pillow rocks all the way down. At low water it's too low, at high water it's crazy, and when the water is just right it is not to be taken lightly. We play it safe, portaging every bag, pack, and rod for a mile across hill and bog. Then Lee Bremer and Dusan Smetana slip into the river. Peter DeJong and I give them a half-hour to make it through the rapids, then we push off. When I lick my lips, my tongue is dry as toast.

We run the big upper drops cleanly, bashing through high rollers, then eddy out behind a midstream boulder. From here on out there are drops, rocks, and souse holes aplenty, but a straightforward line through the melee beckons. "A walk in the park," DeJong figures, nervously, as we guzzle a quart of water and congratulate ourselves on a textbook start.

That's when the wheels come off. I give the boat a strong forward stroke to reenter a hard current line but misjudge my downstream lean. The canoe responds by jerking violently to starboard. As I'm going over I get a glance at DeJong, high-bracing from the bow, but he knows the goose is cooked. In half a second we're both in the water, the boat between us, out of control.

For a couple of minutes it seems like no big deal. We roller-coaster for 300 yards, but then bigger boulders and nasty ledge drops appear. The canoe suddenly lurches to a stop, pinned against a truck-size rock. The current washes me past the canoe as I make a desperate grab for a gunwale. Upstream, DeJong slips over a ledge and bobs to the surface. My OK sign lets him know I'm unhurt, and he returns it with a grin.

Just then he slams into a subsurface boulder. He hits it hard, the kind of hard in which bones end up on the outside of skin and rescue operations commence. His grin morphs instantly into an O of pain. He slides over a hump of foaming water and comes to an instant stop, his body downstream, right leg pointing upcurrent. The look on DeJong's face is as alarming as his posture, one foot entrapped between rocks on the river bottom as the Missinaibi River pours over his shoulders.

Twenty yards downstream, I can do nothing but watch as he struggles to right himself and keep his head above water. If he loses purchase and his free leg slips, the current will sweep him downstream and break his leg, if it isn't broken already. DeJong strains against the river current, at times completely submerged as he tries to twist his leg out of the snare.

Suddenly he wrenches himself loose. Grimacing, he works across the river, and I gather a rescue rope in case he stumbles again. He makes it to the overturned canoe wild-eyed and panting, soaked and starting to chill. "I'm all right," he says. For a full minute neither of us speaks. "Strange way to catch a walleye, eh?" he says. We laugh the nervous laugh of a couple of guys who know they've dodged a bullet.

—T. EDWARD NICKENS
Field & Stream, "Walleyes Gone Wild," May 2006

PGRADE YOUR
URVIVAL KIT

l survival kit should contain the fundamentals—waterproof matches, whistle, compass, knife, water-purifying tablets, a small flashlight. Think you have all your bases covered? See if you have room for a few of these low-volume lifesavers. —T.E.N.

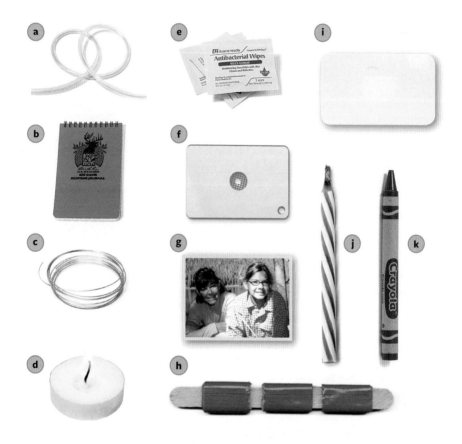

(A) SURGICAL TUBING Use it as a straw to suck water from shallow seeps, as a tourniquet, or as a means to blow a spark to flame. **(B) WATERPROOF PAPER** Leave a note for rescuers—even in a howling blizzard. **(C) WIRE** If you can't think of 10 ways to use this, you're not an outdoorsman to begin with. **(D) TEA LIGHT CANDLE** The longer-burning flame will light wet wood. **(E) ANTIBACTERIAL WIPES** Stave off infection with a single-use packet. **(F) SIGNAL MIRROR** On a clear day, a strong flash can be seen from 10 miles away. **(G) SMALL PHOTO OF LOVED ONES** Thinking of family and friends helps keep survival instincts strong. **(H) BLAZE ORANGE DUCT TAPE WOUND AROUND A TONGUE DEPRESSOR** Tear off 1-inch strips of tape to use as fire starters or route markers. Shave wood with your knife to use as tinder. **(I) FRESNEL LENS** The size of a credit card, this clear lens will start a fire using sunlight. **(J) TRICK BIRTHDAY CANDLES** The wind can't blow them out. **(K) RED CRAYON** Mark trees as you move. You can also use the crayon as a fire starter.

22 START A FIRE WITH YOUR BINOCULARS

It's not easy, but it's not impossible. And if it has come down to this, you're probably running out of options, so there's no harm in giving it a shot.

STEP 1 Disassemble the binoculars and remove one convex objective lens. Gather tinder, a stick to hold the tinder, some kindling, and a Y-shaped twig to hold the lens in place.

STEP 2 Arrange the tinder on the end of the small stick and put this on the ground. Having the tinder slightly elevated will increase airflow and flammability, and having it on the stick will allow you to move it to the area where the sun's rays are most concentrated.

STEP 3 Drive the Y-shaped stick into the ground and settle the lens inside its fork—carving some grooves will help. Focus the smallest point of intensified sunlight onto the tinder. It is critical that this focused beam not wobble. Once the tinder smolders, blow gently, and have larger twigs ready to light. —T.E.N.

23 SWIM WITH YOUR CLOTHES ON

The best strategy for drown-proofing is to stay with your boat. But what if your boat sinks at 4 AM and you go overboard with no hope of help? The best swimming stroke for survival is the breast stroke. It's the only stroke that provides forward vision, which keeps panic at bay, and relies on leg power, which will keep you moving much longer than crawl and side strokes. Here's how:

JUST SWIM! People drown trying to get their shoes off. A breast stroke remains efficient even when you're wearing bulky clothing. Keep your clothes on, roll over on your stomach, and get moving.

MAINTAIN FORWARD MOMENTUM The best way to do this is with an efficient glide. After each pull with your arms, regain an arrow shape with hands one on top of the other, straight out in front, and legs straight behind. As your glide slows, begin the next pull. Try to get a good 3-second count from each glide.

TAILOR YOUR STROKE TO THE CONDITIONS
In cold water especially, take it easy. As long as you retain forward momentum, you won't sink. —T.E.N.

24 SCOUT FOR SHELTER

The fundamental purpose of shelter is to protect your body from the elements. When you're hunting for a prime shelter spot, look for one that does three things: keeps you dry, fends off the wind, and provides shade. Here are some location-scouting tips.

THINK ABOUT TOPOGRAPHY A rock overhang or cave can provide good protection. And you might want to avoid ridges (which tend to be windy) and low-lying land near water (where cold air hovers).

LOOK FOR THE MIDDLE Another good option to look for is a relatively level spot with good drainage located on the middle one-third of a hill. These spots tend to have the most comfortable temperature and, if you're lucky, also block the wind.

CONSIDER CRITTERS Avoid dense brush where bugs live, and opt for sites that are off the ground or behind rock formations—they'll protect you from predators.

—R.J.

25 BEAT BLISTERS WITH DUCT TAPE

STEP 1 Drain the blister with a sterilized needle or knife tip. Insert the tip into the base of the blister, then press out the fluid. Keep the flap of skin intact.

STEP 2 Cut a hole slightly larger than the blister in some pliable cloth. Put a second layer on top and seal this "doughnut bandage" to your foot with duct tape. No duct tape? Then there's little hope for you to begin with. —T.E.N.

26 HOLE UP IN A TREE WELL

Snow is not necessarily an enemy in a blizzard. It's a great insulator, and if you build a proper snow shelter, it'll keep you safe and warm for a short period.

You can quickly make an effective snow shelter in a tree well (the depression in snow around a tree trunk formed by the protective canopy of branches above it).

First, reinforce the natural enclosure by propping up additional branches around the lowest branches. Next, dig out the snow accumulated around the trunk. Finally, lay evergreen boughs on the floor to make a comfortable sleeping place that can be as much as 40º F warmer than the temperature outside.—R.J.

27 SURVIVE ON ACORNS

Stick with acorns from the white oak family (white oak, chestnut oak, bur oak), which have less tannin than red oak nuts. Cull any nuts with a tiny hole in the husk—this is made by an acorn weevil. Remove the cap and shell the rest with a knife or pliers from a multitool.

THE EASY WAY TO EAT ACORNS
To leach out the tannins, tie the nuts in a T-shirt. Submerge it in a running stream for several hours. Taste occasionally to test for bitterness. Or boil the nuts, changing the water frequently until it runs fairly clear. Then roast near a fire. Eat as is or grind into flour.

THE HARD WAY TO EAT ACORNS
Grind or pound shelled acorns, then mix with enough water to create a paste. Place a clean cloth in a wire sieve, scoop the acorn mush on top, and run fresh cold water over the mixture, squeezing water through the mush and out through the sieve. Taste occasionally, until the bitterness is removed. Use as a coarse meal like grits, or pound it into finer flour. —T.E.N.

28 MAKE A FIRE BED

It's freezing, and you're stuck in the woods sans a sleeping bag? Make like a pot roast and construct a life-saving fire bed. Scrape out a gravelike trench in the dirt about 1 foot wide and 8 inches deep. Line it with very dry, egg-size to fist-size stones, if available. (Wet rocks from a stream or lake can explode when heated.)

Next, burn a hot fire into coals and spread a layer in the trench. Cover with at least 4 inches of dirt and tamp down with your boot. Wait one hour. If the ground warms in less than an hour, add more dirt. Now spread out a ground sheet of canvas, plastic, or spare clothing. Check the area twice for loose coals that could ignite your makeshift mattress. Ease onto your fire bed and snooze away. —T.E.N.

29 TIE A HUNTER'S BEND

Unlike most knots, the hunter's bend is relatively new, invented only in the 20th century. It's perfect for joining two ropes, of either equal or dissimilar diameters, which makes it perfect for survival situations when odd scraps of cordage might be all you have at hand. And it's a great knot to use with slick synthetic ropes. —T.E.N.

1 Lay the two lines side by side, with tag ends in opposite directions.

4 Push the rear working end through the middle of both loops.

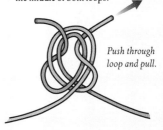

Push through loop and pull.

2 Loop the lines, making sure neither rope twists on top of the other.

Keep lines from twisting.

5 Seat the knot by holding the standing parts firmly and pulling both working ends. Pull the standing parts in opposite directions.

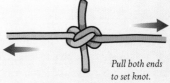

Pull both ends to set knot.

3 Bring the front working end around behind the loops and up through the center.

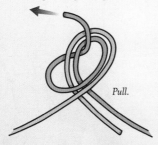

Pull.

30 MAKE A BLOWGUN

Drop your squirrel rifle in the river? It's time to channel your inner aboriginal and hunt squirrels with a blowgun and darts fletched with thistle.

STEP 1 Cut a piece of river cane 6 to 8 feet long. If necessary, straighten it by heating the bent parts over a fire and bending until straight. Leave it to dry in the sun for a week.

STEP 2 To remove the solid joints, heat the end of a straight steel rod until it's red-hot and burn out the joints inside your cane. Repeat until the cane is hollow. Smooth the bore by wrapping the steel rod with sandpaper and sanding the interior joints smooth. The smoother the bore, the faster the dart will fly.

STEP 3 To make a dart (opposite page), whittle a hardwood shaft to about 12 inches long and 3/16 inch in diameter. Then, whittle a sharp point on one end.

STEP 4 Tie a 2-foot string to the dart's blunt end. Hold a bundle of bull thistle or cotton against the blunt end, hold the end of the string taut in your mouth, and roll the dart shaft so that the thistle or cotton is held tight to the shaft but is still fluffy enough to form a fletching larger than the inside diameter of the blowgun. Tie off the string. —T.E.N.

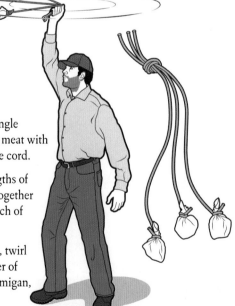

31 FLING A BOLA

Hey, if David took down Goliath with a single stone, you ought to be able to collect some meat with three handfuls of rocks and some parachute cord.

STEP 1 Tie the ends of three 40-inch lengths of parachute cord (or other 3/8-inch roping) together with an overhand knot. Secure a small pouch of rocks to each free end.

STEP 2 Take hold of the bola by the knot, twirl it over your head, and chuck this messenger of death into a flock of low-flying ducks, ptarmigan, or other, similar birds. —T.E.N.

32 SPLIT A LOG WITH A KNIFE

A knife is no replacement for an ax when it comes to rendering firewood. Still, you can use a hunting knife to expose the dry interior of a damp log by pounding the back of the blade with a wood baton.

Make several shingles this way, splitting thin, U-shaped wooden slices from the side of a round of firewood. Angle the edges of the shingles to make wedges and then insert the wedges into an existing lengthwise crack in a log. (If there isn't one, create one with your blade.) Hammer the wedges with a wood baton to split the log end-to-end and expose more surface for burning. —K.M.

33 USE SUPERGLUE TO CLOSE A WOUND

So-called "superglues" were used in the Vietnam War to close wounds and stem bleeding. Dermabond, a medical formulation, is a slightly different composition that minimizes skin irritation, but as many an outdoorsman will attest, plain ol' superglue will hold a cut together better than a strip bandage, and instances of irritation are rare. If you're stuck in the backcountry with no other way to close a wound, this will get you through until you can get to a doctor. Always use an unopened tube of glue. Clean the cut and pinch it shut.

Next, you'll want to dab a drop or two of superglue directly on the incision and then spread it along the length of the cut with something clean. The bandage is watertight and will seal out infecting agents. —T.E.N.

34 GENERATE YOUR OWN TINDER

So, you can't find any handy dry tinder, and you forgot to pack in your own for emergencies. Never fear! You can make your own with a fire plough. Cut a groove in piece of soft wood, then rub the tip of a slightly harder shaft up and down the groove. The friction will push out a fine sort of sawdust, which will ignite as the temperature increases. —K.M.

Tinder ignites as temperature rises.

35 BUILD A FIRE ON SNOW

Go through the ice, over the bow, or into a blizzard and you'll need a fire—fast and before your fleece and fingers freeze. Let's assume you're not a complete moron: You have a workable lighter. Here's how to spark an inferno no matter how much snow is on the ground.

STEP 1 Start busting brush. You'll need a two-layer fire platform of green, wrist-thick (or larger) branches to raft your blaze above deep snow cover. Lay down a row of 3-foot-long branches and then another perpendicular row on top. Stay away from overhanging boughs; rising heat will melt snow trapped in foliage.

STEP 2 Lay out the fuel and don't scrimp on this step. Collect and organize plenty of dry tinder and kindling and twice as many large branches as you think you'll need. Super-dry tinder is critical. Birch bark, pine needles, wood shavings, pitch splinters, cattail fluff, and the dead, dry twigs from the sheltered lower branches of conifers are standards. Place tinder between your hands and rub vigorously to shred the material. You'll need a nest as least as large as a Ping-Pong ball. Pouring rain and snow? Think creatively: dollar bills, pocket lint, fuzzy wool, and a snipped piece of shirt fabric will work.

STEP 3 Take a little bit of time (not too much!) to plan the fire so it dries out wet wood as it burns. Place a large branch or dry rock across the back of the fire and arrange wet wood across the fire a few inches above the flame. Don't crisscross; laying the wood parallel will aid the drying process.

—T.E.N.

36 DRINK YOUR OWN URINE

Aron Ralston, the climber who amputated his arm with a pocketknife when he was pinned under a boulder, sipped his own urine during his ordeal. And while no one can say for sure whether it kept him alive, it didn't kill him. (Although it eroded his gums and palate.) If you find yourself in such a desperate fix, here's how to sip safely.

STEP 1 Morning urine may have more concentrated salts and other undesirable compounds. Avoid drinking this batch.

STEP 2 Treat urine with a water filter if available.

STEP 3 Take small sips. —T.E.N.

37 SPIT-ROAST THAT BUNNY

A caveman and cowboy movie cliché, spit roasting is one of the simplest cooking methods. For the spit, choose wood like green oak or hickory that won't give a bad taste to the food. Ideally, the stick has a fork at one end that you can use for turning. Sharpen the other end to push through the meat.

Shave the middle to flatten it along two opposite sides (this prevents the stick from rotating inside the food, so you're rotating the meat, not just the stick). Baste with drippings caught in a pan or on some bark.—R.J.

START A FIRE

BURNING SENSATIONS Always have a couple of these D.I.Y. options on hand. —T.E.N.

INNER TUBE Three-inch strips or squares of bicycle inner tube burn with a rank, smoky flame hot enough to dry small kindling. No bike? Try the rubber squares in a wader-patch kit (don't forget the flammable patch glue) or a slice from a boot insole.

DUCT TAPE A fist-size ball of loosely wadded duct tape is easy to light and will burn long enough to dry out tinder and kindling.

EMERGENCY FLARE Cut a 2- to 4-inch section from an emergency road flare and seal the end with wax. It's easily lit even with wet gloves on.

DRYER LINT Collect enough dryer lint to fill a gallon-size resealable bag halfway. Add ⅛ cup of citronella lamp fuel and squish it around to mix thoroughly.

EGG CARTON AND SAWDUST Stuff each opening in a cardboard egg carton about half full of sawdust (collect this from your local school wood shop) and then add melted paraffin wax. Mix, let cool, and break apart.

COTTON BALLS AND PETROLEUM JELLY It's a Boy Scout standby because it works. Stuff petroleum jelly–soaked cotton balls into a film canister or waterproof pill bottle and you have several minutes of open flame at the ready.

NATURAL WONDERS Learn to identify and gather natural tinder in your neck of the woods.

CEDAR BARK Common cedar bark should be worked over with a rock to smash the fibers. Pull the strands apart with your fingers, and roll the material back and forth between your hands.

BIRCH BARK The flammable oils in the papery bark of birches make this a time-tested fire catcher. Strip ribbons of bark from downed trees; it works just as well as bark from live ones.

SPANISH MOSS Not a moist moss, at all, but an epiphytic, or "air plant," Spanish moss is a great tinder. But don't carry it around; it's notorious for harboring chiggers.

TINDER FUNGUS In northern areas, look for bulbous blotches of blackish wood on live birch trees. The inside of the fungus, which is reddish-brown, easily catches a spark. Crumble it for a quick start to a fire or use chunks of it to keep a coal alive.

CATTAIL FLUFF The cottony interior of a cattail spike can be fluffed into a spark-catching blaze. Have more tinder nearby, because cattail fluff burns out quickly.

SAGEBRUSH BARK Pound strips of bark with a rock and then shred them between your palms and fashion a tinder basket.

PUNK WOOD Rotten, dry wood will flame up with just a few sparks. Use a knife blade held at 90 degrees to file off punk dust, and have larger pieces handy to transfer the sparks to larger punk wood that will burn with a coal.

39 SKIN AND COOK A SNAKE

Mr. No Shoulders might give you the willies, but a hot meal of snake meat might also give you enough energy to make it back to civilization. This should be a last resort, as some of these creatures are protected.

STEP 1 Cut off the snake's head. Insert the knife tip into the anal vent and run the blade all the way up the belly.

STEP 2 Free a section of the skin. Grasp the snake in one hand, the freed skin section in the other, and pull apart.

STEP 3 Remove all of the entrails, which lie along the base of the spine.

STEP 4 Chop into bite-size pieces. Fry or boil. —T.E.N.

40 NAVIGATE BY DELIBERATE OFFSET

Say you climb a big hill to glass prime elk country. Now you have to bushwhack back, and even though it's no big deal to find the trail, moving in a straight line will be difficult. So, which way do you turn on the lakeshore or trail to find your original location?

Figure it out by using deliberate offset: Add or subtract about 10 degrees to your required compass bearing. Each degree of offset will move your arrival about 20 yards to the right or left for every 1,000 yards traveled. Hoof it back to the trail, and you'll know that you're off to one side. No guesswork. Make the turn. —T.E.N.

Poison Ivy

Poison Sumac

41 STEER CLEAR OF POISONOUS PLANTS

Really, who likes getting poked and stung while beating their way through the bush? To protect your skin against thorns and stinging nettles, wear long pants and long sleeves, and don leather gloves that'll let you move plants aside with ease. Use a long stick to open up a path through a thicket, and employ your well-shod feet to mash plants down out of your way. But if you can identify a plant as poisonous, don't walk through it; the itch-inducing resin collects on your clothing and boots, and might eventually get transferred to your skin. —R.J.

Poison Oak

42 ATTRACT RESCUERS WITH SMOKE

A large plume of smoke can attract rescue attention better than any other method. Two basics: Unless you have plenty of energy and fuel, don't waste either maintaining a signal fire. Keep three fires ready to light when you spot a rescue plane. But don't waste matches trying to light a signal fire with a single match. Instead, ignite a longer-burning super-match. Look around: soda straws, plastic spoons, strips of rubber, and twists of duct tape all burn long and hot. Once lit, bring this super-match to bear on the signal fires.

Black smoke is usually better than white because it won't be mistaken for a campfire. Test green vegetation to make sure it produces plenty of smoke. To really pour out dark, billowing plumes, feed your blaze with anything petroleum-based: tires, oily rags, truck floor mats, and boat cushions.

White smoke is often more visible in country full of conifers. Feed wet foliage into the fire to produce white smoke. To make a large, billowing plume, build a big fire, and then nearly smother it with wet leaves or grass.

Try to build your fire in an opening where it can be seen easily from the air.

—T.E.N.

43 STAY SAFE IN A CAVE

Like any neighborhood, a cave has its advantages and disadvantages. Before you can move in, you need to make sure it isn't already occupied. Depending on where you are, caves might be favored dwellings for venomous snakes, bats, wolves, bears, cougars—you get the picture. Even if the only cave dwellers are rats, mice, or squirrels, you might become ill from contact with hantavirus in their urine or feces, so look for a clean cave floor. One other caution: Caves exist because the ceiling "caved" in from some type of erosion. If you see evidence of instability overhead or fresh rockfalls on the floor, or if there's water flowing through the cave, it's probably not structurally sound, and the wisest choice is probably to move on.—R.J.

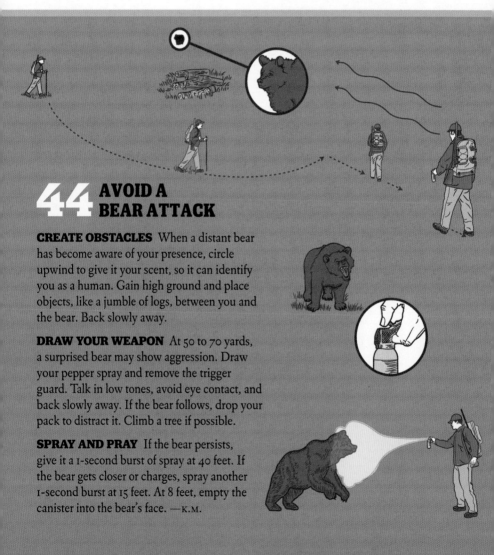

44 AVOID A BEAR ATTACK

CREATE OBSTACLES When a distant bear has become aware of your presence, circle upwind to give it your scent, so it can identify you as a human. Gain high ground and place objects, like a jumble of logs, between you and the bear. Back slowly away.

DRAW YOUR WEAPON At 50 to 70 yards, a surprised bear may show aggression. Draw your pepper spray and remove the trigger guard. Talk in low tones, avoid eye contact, and back slowly away. If the bear follows, drop your pack to distract it. Climb a tree if possible.

SPRAY AND PRAY If the bear persists, give it a 1-second burst of spray at 40 feet. If the bear gets closer or charges, spray another 1-second burst at 15 feet. At 8 feet, empty the canister into the bear's face. —K.M.

45 TREAT A SNAKEBITE

Snake bites happen all the time. And even a bite from a so-called harmless snake can cause infection or an allergic reaction. If you're bitten, the best course of action is to get emergency medical assistance as soon as you can. In the meantime, do the following:

STEP ONE Wash the bite with soap and water.

STEP TWO Immobilize the bitten area and, if possible, keep it lower than the heart.

STEP THREE Cover the area with a clean, cool compress or a moist dressing to minimize swelling and discomfort.

STEP FOUR Monitor vital signs, such as temperature and pulse rate.

STEP FIVE If you can't reach emergency medical care within 30 minutes, place a suction device over the bite to help draw venom up out of the wound. You should only use your mouth to suck out the venom as a last resort—and then, be sure to spit it out. Then wrap a bandage 2 to 4 inches (4–10 cm) above the bite to help slow the venom's movement. Don't totally cut off circulation—the bandage should be loose enough that you can slip a finger under it.—R.J.

46 FILTER WATER WITH YOUR PANTS

Yes, you can use a bag if you have one, but a cut-off pant leg makes a great water filter. Modesty must give way to survival, so don't be shy about making the most of your denim: Rescuers won't care if they find you wandering around in short shorts. To turn a pant leg into a filter, tie off the bottom and add alternating layers of gravel and sand to trap particles of debris. Slowly add water to the top of the filter, allowing it to trickle down through the layers into a catch basin. The water in this basin is ready for the next step in the purification process—boiling.

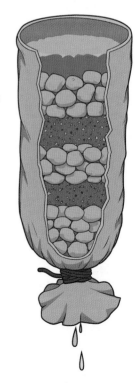

DO allow cloudy water to settle before filtering or chemically treating it. If water is cold, wait at least 30 minutes after chemical treatment before drinking.

DON'T drink from a stagnant pool of water where there are dead animals around—the water may have poisoned them. Safe water should also support plant life, so look for greenery. Don't consider "wild" water to be safe for consumption until you've treated it.—R.J.

47 LEARN FIRE-MAKING BASICS

Where there's smoke there's fire? Not always, as someone nursing a poorly constructed fire finds out quickly. But if you want a steady blaze to cook on, keep animals away, or just warm up, follow these tips:

STEP ONE Prepare a spot with protection from wind and precipitation on dry ground (or a dry platform built up on moist ground).

STEP TWO You need three types of dry fuel: tinder, kindling, and larger pieces of wood. When you think of tinder, imagine a bird's nest, and bundle dry grasses into a nest shape. Kindling can range from the diameter of a matchstick up to the size of a wood pencil, so use splintered wood or small dry twigs snapped off a tree, or shave pencil-size twigs into "fuzz sticks." For the larger pieces of wood, look for dry branches somewhere between the size of your finger and the size of your forearm. Shattered or split wood is best.

STEP THREE In a fire pit, build a tepee of kindling and place the tinder bundle beneath it. Don't construct it too tightly, as the fire needs space to breathe. Have the larger pieces of wood close so they're handy when the fire is ready.

STEP FOUR Kneel by the tinder and kindling, using your body as a windbreak. Light the tinder and feed kindling into the fire until you have a strong blaze, then start adding the smallest wood first, working up to the larger pieces. —R.J.

48 MAKE A BOW DRILL

Of all the friction fire-starting methods, the bow drill is the most efficient at maintaining the speed and pressure needed to produce a coal and the easiest to master. The combination of the right fireboard and spindle is the key to success, so experiment with different dry softwoods until you find a set that produces. Remember that the drill must be as hard as or slightly harder than the fireboard.

STEP 1 Cut a notch at the edge of a round impression bored into the fireboard, as you would for a hand drill. Loosely affix the string to a stick bow, which can be any stout wood.

STEP 2 Place the end of a wood drill about the diameter of your thumb into the round impression. Bear down on the drill with a socket (a wood block or stone with a hollow ground into it), catch the drill in a loop of the bowstring, and then vigorously saw back and forth until the friction of the spinning drill produces a coal.

STEP 3 Drop the glowing coal into a bird's nest of fine tinder, lift the nest in your cupped hands, and lightly blow until it catches fire. —K.M.

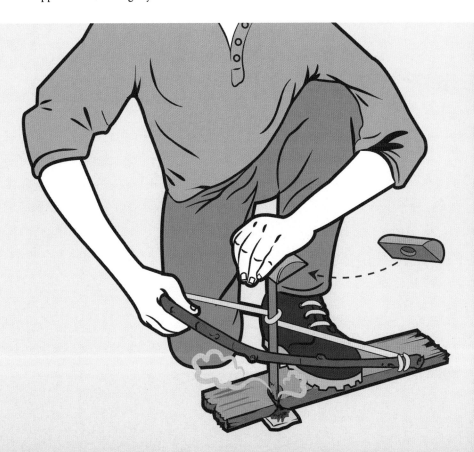

49 SURVIVE A FRIGID DUNKING

An adult has a 50-50 chance of surviving for 50 minutes in 50-degree F water. In some parts of the United States and Canada, that's summertime water temperature. Go overboard in frigid water, and your first challenge is to live long enough to worry about hypothermia.

COLD SHOCK Hit cold water quickly and your body takes an involuntary few gasps of breath followed by up to three minutes of hyperventilation. You can literally drown while floating, before you have the chance to freeze to death. Keep your face out of the water. Turn away from waves and spray. If you're not wearing a personal flotation device (PFD), float on your back until you catch your breath. Don't panic. Cold shock passes after a minute or two. Only then can you plot your next steps.

HYPOTHERMIA The more of your body that you can manage to get out of the water, the better. Crawl up on anything that floats. Also, the more you flail around, the more your body will actually cool off. Unless you plan to swim to safety, stay still.

HELP Assume the heat-escape-lessening posture, also known as HELP. Hold your arms across your chest, with your upper arms pressed firmly against your sides; and your legs pulled up as far toward your chest as you can. This buffers the core areas of your chest, armpits, and groin. Remember that you can also lose a lot of body heat through your head, so try and find your hat if at all possible. The ultimate decision is whether to float or swim. Your ability to swim is severely hampered in cold water. Swimming increases the rate of heat loss up to 50 percent. It should be considered a last resort for rescue. —T.E.N.

50 SWING A MEAN MACHETE

While a machete is fun for pretending to fight off a band of ninjas, it can also be quite useful. You can wield one to chop and split wood, or to clear vines and grasses from the trail ahead.

As with any cutting tool, the most important thing is to prevent injury to yourself. Always consider where the blade would end up if it missed its target, and make sure no part of your body is in that location. Grip the machete handle firmly, swing deliberately, and be ready to react if the blade glances off or misses. Keep the blade sharp and don't let the edge strike the ground, or it will become dull. If you're clearing vegetation, use a side-to-side sweeping action, and feel free to make lots of kung fu noises as you go. —R.J.

51 BUILD A ONE-MATCH FIRE WHEN YOUR LIFE DEPENDS ON IT

If things are so bad that you're down to one match, then it's no time for you to be taking chances. The secret to last-chance fire building is attention to detail long before the match comes out of your pocket.

STEP 1 Begin with tinder. Collect three times as much as you think you'll need; don't stop looking until you have a double handful. Shred it well; what you're going for is a fiberlike consistency.

Conifer pitch, pine needles, cedar bark, birch bark, and dry bulrushes all make excellent natural tinder. Lots of other common items make good fire-starting material, too. Turn your pockets inside out to look for lint or candy bar wrappers. Duct tape burns like crazy; maybe there's a strip stuck to your gun case. Wader patch glue and plastic arrow fletching will work, too. The more variety you have, the longer the burn.

STEP 2 Gather twice as much kindling as you think you're going to need, and separate it into piles of like-size pieces. If you have to stop what you're doing and fumble for a pencil-size piece of pine at the wrong moment, your fire will go up in smoke. Your piles should consist pieces the diameter of a red wiggler, of a .22 cartridge, and of a 20-gauge shell. Use a knife to fuzz up the outer edges of a few sticks for a quicker catch.

STEP 3 Start small. Use two-thirds of your tinder to begin with and save the other third in case you need a second try with the dying embers of your first shot. Arrangement is important: You want to be able to get your match head near the bottom of the pile, and you also want to ensure that the slightest breeze pushes emerging flames toward your materials. Blow gently and feed only the fast-burning flames. —T.E.N.

52 KEEP BUGS OUT OF YOUR PANTS

Even one bug bite can be too many—especially when you're in a wet environment, where the infection risk is high and the availability of calamine lotion is low.

To keep bugs from crawling into your sleeves and pant legs, fold under the cuffs, then tie something around them. You can use shoelaces or elastic blousing bands, available at military surplus stores. The cuff straps sported by commuter cyclists everywhere are also a good bet; you can find them in bike shops. And as in so many other situations, duct tape will do the trick in a pinch. —R.J.

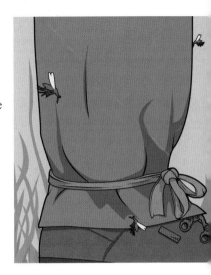

53 CHOKE DOWN BUGS

A fistful of bugs for dinner might seem a little crazy. And good? Not so much. But when the chips are down, this is the original MRE (meal, ready to eat), packed with enough nutritional punch to help get you through the night. The average grasshopper sports 20.6 grams of protein and 5 milligrams of iron—that's twice the iron and just 3 grams of protein less than a similar spoonful of lean ground beef. The FDA allows one rodent feces per sampling of popcorn. Wouldn't you rather eat a hopper?

START WITH THE LEGS Remove the grasshopper's legs to help control the bug and keep it from hanging up in your gullet. Some grasshopper gourmets remove the head by grasping the thorax and slowly pulling off the head. This pulls out much of the entrails, and the rest can be scraped away with a stick.

COOK BEFORE EATING Cooking is critical to kill internal parasites. Skewer insects on a thin stick and hold the stick over a fire, or roast the grasshoppers on a rock set close to the flame. A grasshopper is just like any other small piece of meat. In fact, once you get over the bug phobia, that's exactly what it is. —T.E.N.

54 MAKE A TRAP OR DIE TRYING

Compared to the hours of energy expended while foraging or hunting in a survival situation, traps take little time to set, and, unlike firearms or fishing rods, they work for you while you sleep. But to trap animals with enough regularity to feed yourself, you need to heed these three principles as you set up.

1. LOCATION Rabbits, muskrats, groundhogs, and other animals make distinct trails that they use over and over. These trails are the best places to set traps, but they can be difficult to see in bright sunlight. Search for them early or late in the day when the shadows that define them are growing longer.

2. DIRECTION Where possible, narrow an existing trail—by brushing vegetation or driving a couple of small sticks into the ground—to direct the animal into the trap, or place a horizontal stick at the top of the snare so that the animal must duck slightly, ensuring that its head will go right into the noose.

3. SIZE Scale your trap correctly for what you're trying to catch. As a rule, the noose should be one and a half times the diameter of the head of the animal you wish to capture and made of material that will break should you inadvertently snare, say, a cougar's foot.

The most important tool you can carry if you're planning on catching your dinner is a spool of snare wire (26 gauge will be about right for all-purpose small-game snares; use 28 gauge for squirrels, 24 or heavier for beaver-size animals). Soft single-strand wire is superior to nylon monofilament because it holds its shape and game can't chew through it. You can also make snares from braided fishing superlines or 550 parachute cord, depending on the kind of trap you're making.

SQUIRREL SNARE Make a small loop by wrapping the snare wire around a pencil-diameter stick twice and then turning the stick to twist the wire strands together. Pass the long wire end through the loop to form the snare (a). To build a squirrel snare, attach a series of small wire snares around a long stick propped against a tree (b). You can catch several squirrels at a time with this setup.

TWITCH-UP SNARE Tie a small overhand loop knot in your parachute cord. Then fold the loop back on itself to form Mickey Mouse ears and weave the tag end through the ears (a). To build the twitch-up snare, use more cord to tie a spring pole or the branch of a small tree in tension (b). Set up a trigger mechanism like the one shown (c). When the animal's head goes through the loop, the trigger is released, and it snatches the animal into the air, out of reach of other predators. —K.M.

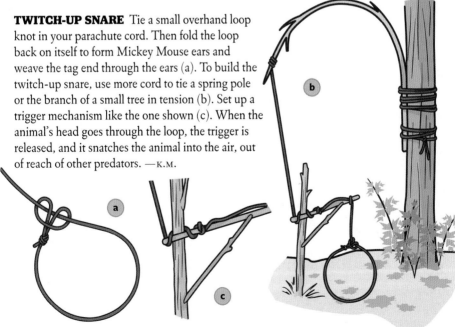

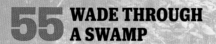

55 WADE THROUGH A SWAMP

The best way to navigate a swamp is on an airboat. Don't have one of those? Well, then—you'll just have to walk and wade.

BEWARE THE WATER Stay out of it as much as possible. If the wet route looks like your only option, observe the wildlife before wading or swimming. If the ibis won't go there, you shouldn't either. Watch for crocs and alligators, and don't forget serpents: Venomous snakes and deadly constrictors live in and near water.

NAVIGATE CAREFULLY It's easy to get lost with everything looking alike, so pick the direction you believe to be toward safety, and maintain that heading, deviating only to avoid obstacles. Before going around something, check your heading and pick a fixed point on the other side to walk toward. It will be easier to get back on course quickly.

DON'T GET STUCK Swamp mud and silt can be extremely sticky and deep, and underwater root tangles can trap your feet. Quicksand likely won't kill you, but it can slow you down. Carry a long pole to check water depth and to probe the ground ahead before you take a step. Peat bogs amplify these risks, as they're deeper and contain a thick tangle of vegetation that will trap you. Simply walk around them instead. —R.J.

56 BUILD A SHELTER FROM BRANCHES AND LEAVES

If you can't find an enclosure like a cave or an overhang, use brush and branches to build a leafy lean-to.

STEP ONE To make a roof beam, cut a log that's 2 to 3 feet longer than your body. Remove its limbs.

STEP TWO Locate a tree with a low branch, and prop one end of the beam in the crotch—ideally, it should be about 4 feet from the ground. If you can't find a low branch, lash the beam between trees that are 6 to 8 feet apart. And if you can't find the right trees, use stumps or boulders or anything else that can serve to support the beam off the ground. Remember, you don't need to be able to stand up inside the shelter, and keeping the beam (and therefore the roof) low to the ground makes the space easier to heat with your body warmth.

STEP THREE Build a roof by leaning smaller limbs at angles against the center beam. These rafters span the space from the beam to the ground. If possible, lash the angled rafters to the beam for greater strength.

STEP FOUR For more insulation, weave lightweight limbs through the rafters. (Weaving them will keep them from sliding down or being blown off by the wind.) Once you've constructed a fairly tight roof, add insulation by piling on bark pieces, leaves, pine needles, or other small debris you find scattered around the area.

STEP FIVE Insulate the floor of the shelter with leaves or other soft matter to make it more comfortable. If you're going to sleep on the ground, you might as well make it as pleasant as possible.

—R.J.

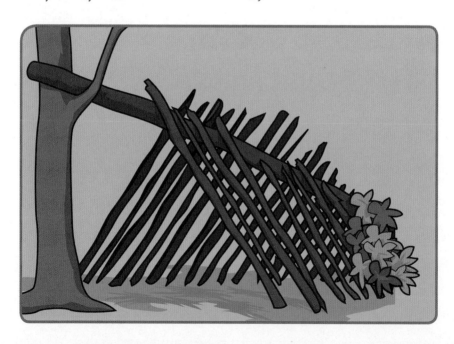

57 MAKE A BED IN A PINCH

Too posh to sleep in a garbage bag? Not if you want to stay dry. A large plastic trash bag can serve as a waterproof body covering. For insulation, stuff the bag with leaves, pine needles, and dry grasses. —R.J.

58 CUT SAPLINGS FOR SHELTER

If you find yourself in need of a shelter, you can gather the wood to construct one by felling a tree. If you can bend a green sapling, you can cut it, but it helps if you bend the trunk back and forth several times to weaken the wood fibers before bringing your knife to bear on it. To cut a sapling, hold it bent with one hand and then press down on the outside of the curve with your knife blade angled slightly (a). Rock the blade as you cut, while maintaining steady downward pressure (b). Support the trunk as you work to keep it from splintering, which would make it difficult for you to finish the cut. —K.M.

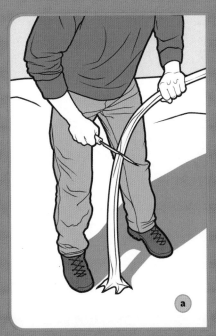

Bend the sapling to make the cut easier.   *Use straight downward force.*

59 MEASURE REMAINING DAYLIGHT

Setting up camp in the dark is no picnic. To help you decide whether you're better off continuing to hike or stopping to set up camp, estimate how much time is left until sundown. Hold your hand at arm's length with your fingers positioned horizontally between the horizon and the sun. The width of each finger between the sun and the horizon is roughly equal to 15 minutes before sunset. —R.J.

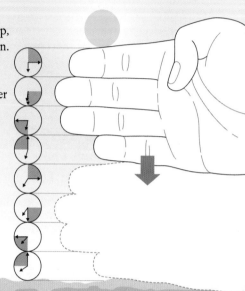

60 TRACK BACK WITH A GPS UNIT

Most people treat their GPS unit as though it were some some kind of digital toaster with a 100-page instruction manual. Which is to say, they use it only for the most basic tasks it's capable of. Most never realize that the track-log and track-back functions of most popular GPS units, however, are just the ticket for outdoorsmen who want to figure out how to return to a truck or cabin from a distant tree stand or duck blind. Here's how it works.

STEP 1 Turn on the GPS unit, leave it on, and leave it out where it can get a clear signal.

STEP 2 Activate the unit's track-log function. (Look for a menu choice called "Tracks" or "Trails.") Don't customize the settings, such as choosing how often the unit plots a waypoint. These will already be preset to monitor your rate of movement and lay down electronic crumbs at just the right time.

STEP 3 At your final destination, stop the track log and store and name the track before powering off. You can now easily follow that track back the way you came with your unit's return feature, or even download it to GPS mapping software. —T.E.N.

61 DESCEND A CLIFF WITH A SINGLE ROPE

If you have to rappel down a cliff with a single rope, you won't get a second chance to do it right. Take notes.

CHOOSE AN ANCHOR POINT This can be a sturdy tree or rock outcrop near the edge of the precipice. Make sure the anchor point won't pinch the rope as you pull it down from below. Pass the rope around the anchor so that the two ends are even and meet the landing point with a few feet of extra rope.

WRAP YOUR BODY With your back to the cliff, straddle the double strand of rope. Pass it around your right hip and then across your chest and over your left shoulder. Grasp the ropes at your lower back with your right hand, and bring them around to your right hip. With your left hand, grasp the ropes in front at chest height.

DESCEND Keeping close to perpendicular to the cliff, walk down the precipice. Relax your grips periodically to slide down the rope. To arrest a swift descent, grip tightly with your right hand while pulling the rope to the front of your waist. At the bottom, retrieve the rope by pulling one end. —T.E.N.

62 IDENTIFY EDIBLE INSECTS

Don't be deceived by their less-than-delicious appearance: Some bugs are edible, while others contain toxins. These are your safest bets:

ANTS These trail snacks taste like lemon drops, thanks to the formic acid in their systems. Just pop them in your mouth and chew—unless it's a fire ant, a bullet ant, or another ant that bites. Avoid those!

GRUBS Beetle larvae are fine to eat plain and live or, if you want to be fancy, as an addition to soup.

GRASSHOPPERS Skewer grasshoppers on a thin stick and roast them over the coals of your campfire.

SCORPIONS Pin the critter down with a knife, cut off its claws and stinger, and roast or toss in soup.

BEETLES Some are edible; some will make you sick. Don't eat them unless you gain local knowledge first.—R.J.

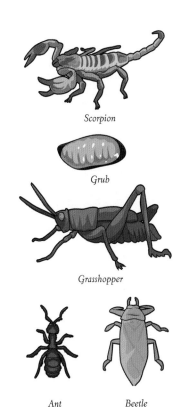

Scorpion

Grub

Grasshopper

Ant   *Beetle*

63 PREDICT THE WEATHER WITH PLANTS

Plants can tip you off that rain is on the way, usually because parts of them close as the moisture content in the air increases. (They don't want rain washing away their precious pollen reserves.) The plants here show their typical appearances on dry days (on the left) and rainy ones (on the right); look for these cues to avoid getting drenched.—R.J.

Shamrock

Chicory

Morning Glory

64 DIG A HOLE TRAP

Another way to catch an animal is to dig a hole 3 feet deep with an opening as big as your fist and walls that get wider toward the bottom. Lay a small log, elevated slightly by stones or other debris, over the top of the hole. With any luck, a critter will scurry under the log for cover and fall into the hole, and the hole's sloped walls will prevent it from climbing out.—R.J.

65 NAVIGATE TALL GRASS

Tall grass poses two problems: If the grass is taller than your head, you can't see where you're going. In that case, you have to navigate by compass.

The other problem is that living things hide in tall grass: snakes, insects, spiders, and predators. Carry a walking staff and use it to probe the area ahead. Make noise to alert animals of your approach. Wear long sleeves, long pants, high boots (or tuck your pants into your boots), gloves, and a hat to protect against bugs and bites.—R.J.

66 TIE A SQUARE LASHING

When you need to build a temporary structure in a hurry, in virtually every possible situation, the knot you'll want to go with is the versatile and easy-to-tie square lashing: It's a quick and an effective way to secure two posts together.

STEP ONE Cross the the first set of poles that you're using to build your structure. Wrap the rope around the bottom post, with the active end—the end that you'll be looping around the poles—on top. Leave yourself a fair amount of rope on the active end.

STEP TWO Wrap the active end around the post, threading it under the first wrap. (This is called a clove hitch, and it's the basis of your knot.)

STEP THREE Twist the static end around the rope's active end. Then weave

the active end around the posts, wrapping so the rope goes behind the vertical post, over the horizontal post, and under the vertical post again.

STEP FOUR Repeat this wrap two more times, pulling on the rope to tighten as you go.

STEP FIVE Wrap the rope so that it now crosses in front of the vertical post and behind the horizontal one. Repeat several times.

STEP SIX When your knot is sturdy enough, tie it off with a clove hitch, wrapping the active end once around the horizontal pole to make a loop, then looping around the pole again and threading it through the first loop. Repeat with each set of poles until your structure is complete.—R.J.

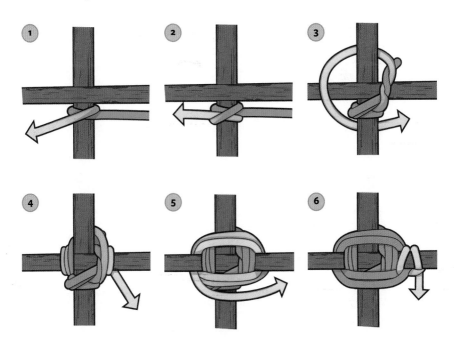

67 MAKE A FIRE FOUR WAYS

You're lost in the woods. It's getting cold and dark, and like a big idiot, you seem to have left your survival kit at home. Never fear! Even if you don't have matches or a lighter, you can still spark a blaze with the right tools and techniques. Be sure to have your tinder bundle, kindling, and fuel wood ready before you start.—R.J.

FIRE PLOW No string for a bow? Friction between a board and a plow can do the trick. Carve a central groove in the board and rub a branch rapidly up and down inside this trough. It's more work than a bow drill, and it takes longer, but you can still make a coal.

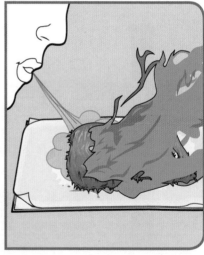

STEEL WOOL AND A BATTERY Rub the terminals of a battery against raw steel wool (not a Brillo pad). Keep at it, and electrical resistance will cause the steel wool to glow red hot. Once it does, move it to your pile of tinder and kindling, and blow the pile into flame.

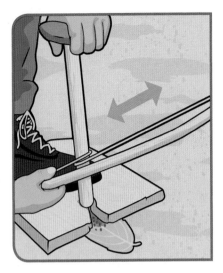
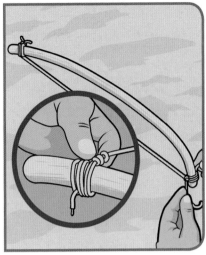

BOW DRILL METHOD Notch a board or a flat piece of bark. To make a bow, stretch a string between the ends of a flexible branch and tie it in place, then use a second stick as a vertical spindle. Place the spindle inside the bow with one end in the notched base. Turn the bow once to loop the string around the spindle, then hold the spindle's other end in place with a stone. Place a leaf under the notch and saw back and forth to create a coal. Then move it to the tinder bundle, and blow gently into flame.

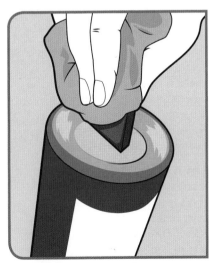

CHOCOLATE AND A SODA CAN Use cheap, waxy chocolate to polish the bottom of a soda can until it gleams like a mirror. Angle it to reflect sunlight onto the tinder bundle (no ordinary flashlight ray will do) and, with luck, the focused light will ignite a flame.

Peak

Peak

You Are Here

0.5 km
1:15 000
1:25 000
0.5
0.1
1/20000/cm=200m
1/10000/cm=100m

68 FIND YOURSELF ON A MAP

FIRST THINGS FIRST: To use a map and compass successfully, you have to figure out where you are on that map. Or to put it in outdoor geek terms, you need to triangulate a "fix" on your position.

KNOW WHICH WAY'S UP Maps are printed with north at the top. Using the compass, orient the map so it aligns with magnetic north.

FIND KEY LANDMARKS Once you have the map oriented, look around you for terrain features like a lake, river, or mountain peak. Identify the same features on the map.

PLOT A COURSE Looking up with your compass in hand, point the red arrow of the compass's base plate (this is called

"shooting a bearing" in orienteering speak) at the visible terrain feature. If the compass shows a bearing of, say, 320 degrees, draw a line from that feature on the map at an angle of 140 degrees (320 minus 180). You are somewhere on that line, called a line of position (LOP).

LAY A FOUNDATION You don't know where you are on that line until you shoot another bearing, preferably at something between 60 and 120 degrees from the first one. When you draw the second LOP on the map, extend it so it crosses the first one. Where the two LOPs intersect is your "fix." That's where you are. Once you know your position, other decisions, such as which way to walk, become much easier. —R.J.

69 UPGRADE YOUR SHELTER

Ducking into a temporary shelter to quickly get out of the elements is one thing, but if you need to live in that ramshackle space for a prolonged period of time, you'll want to make some home improvements.

CALL IN REINFORCEMENTS Use boulders or the upturned root system of downed trees for a basic framework. Gather heavy branches and layer them onto your exterior walls for further protection. If you have a rain poncho or tarp, spread it over the boughs to keep rainwater from pooling inside.

LAY A FOUNDATION Scrape together a deep layer of pine needles or leaves, then add tender boughs to create a soft, insulated floor that's about 8 inches (20 cm) thick. Position logs or stones around the perimeter to hold the floor materials in place. Do the same to a cave floor.

LOOK UP For long stays, you need food storage. You don't want to sleep with that deer carcass, so hang it away from your shelter and out of predators' reach.

LOOK DOWN Go lower in elevation and a healthy distance downwind to dig your latrine, and, if you're sheltering near your water source, make sure to dig at least 100 feet away from it so you don't contaminate your own drinking water.—R.J.

70 BE A BACKCOUNTRY DENTIST

Lose a filling in the backcountry and you might wish you were dead. Make a dental first-aid kit with dental floss, dental wax, cotton pellets, a temporary filling material such as Tempanol, oil of cloves, and a tiny pair of tweezers. To replace a filling, put a few drops of oil of cloves (be careful; it can burn) on a cotton pellet. Use tweezers to place the medicated cotton in the hole, then tamp down with a blade from a multitool. Cover it with the temporary filling material. —T.E.N.

71 BE A MODERN CAVEMAN

There's a reason why bears and other beasts hole up in caves: They're ready-made shelters that provide immediate protection from rain, snow, wind, or brutal sun. No need to work at erecting a hut—just move in and set up housekeeping.

WATCH OUT FOR WATER Make sure the cavern is high enough to be out of danger from flash floods, incoming tides, and storm surges.

PUT UP A FENCE Erect a low stone wall across the opening to help keep dirt from blowing around.

START A FIRE The stone walls make good reflectors for the campfire, and there's no worry of the fire spreading to nearby vegetation and getting out of control. To keep campfire smoke from becoming a problem, build the fire near the cave entrance.

BEAT THE DRAFT Because they are made of rock, caves generally retain the cold. They're good places to escape the heat of a hot desert, but not so desirable in the dead of winter. Unless you can get a good fire going or partition a section of the cavern into a small room, cold air will always surround you. —R.J.

72 MAKE EMERGENCY SNOWSHOES

Walking through deep snow is tough work that will drain you of crucial energy. These snowshoes will help you glide across—not plow through—the snow's surface.

STEP ONE Start by finding two pine boughs with ample foliage, and cutting them to about 3 feet long.

STEP TWO Tie a string near the base of the branch, where you cut it. Then flip the branch over and tie an overhand knot on the opposite side.

STEP THREE Place the branch so that its top (the side that faces upward when the branch is on the tree) is face down in the snow, with the foliage bending upward. Step on it, tie the string to your shoe, and thread the line through the shoelace eyelets.

STEP FOUR Once you're strapped in, just walk across the snow. Your boot will come up from the branch about 30 degrees when you walk, which will keep you from sinking into the snow.—R.J.

73 AVOID DREADED TRENCH FOOT

This malady gets its name from a painful condition many soldiers experienced during World War I, when they stood in the trenches for days and weeks in cold,

waterlogged, filthy boots. Gradually their feet would numb and their skin would turn red or blue. Without treatment, gangrene would set in, leading to amputation. Even today, trench foot impacts unprepared outdoorsmen. Don't be one of its victims.

Prevent the problem by wearing waterproof boots and wool socks. It's also a good idea to shed your boots and socks periodically, air out and massage your feet to promote circulation, and then put on fresh socks if you have them. Your feet will feel better and smell fresher. Best of all, you'll get to keep them.—R.J.

74 BUILD A SWAMP SHELTER

You're in the swamp. The ground is wet. The air is wet. And the vegetation is bloated with water, which makes it a poor building material. As a result, one of the most challenging things to do is erect a dry shelter.

STEP ONE Find a dry spot. Of course, "dry" is relative, but a slight hill should be less wet than areas of lower elevation. It's also a good idea to learn how to spot and avoid run-offs. These sparsely vegetated, eroded spots are prone to flash floods, so they're not ideal for a shelter, especially when rainfall is likely.

STEP TWO Look for a space that's at least a little longer than your body and twice as wide, ideally with four trees at the corners. If you can't find a place with well-spaced trees, try driving sturdy wooden stakes into the ground. (Bamboo works nicely.) A rare benefit of building a shelter in a swamp is that it's relatively easy to plunge stakes into the soggy ground.

STEP THREE Measure and cut branches to build a frame. You'll need two rails that are longer than your body and long enough to connect to your trees or poles. Use a square lashing to secure each rail to the trees or posts. If you don't have rope, gather vines, which you can usually find in most swamp and jungle areas.

STEP FOUR Once the frame is in place, cut shorter branches to lay across the frame as a platform, and tie them to the rails. When you're done, your swamp shelter should be strong enough to hold your full weight, and keep you off the ground and at least somewhat drier.

STEP FIVE For padding and insulation, top off the platform with large leaves or cut sections of moss. And there you've got it: a fairly comfortable bed that's high above the moisture, not to mention beyond the reach of many animals and insects. —R.J.

75 MAXIMIZE HEAT FROM A CAMPFIRE

The problem with campfires is that most of the heat escapes, so the fire warms only the side of your body that faces the flames. The ideal is to build a fire between two reflective surfaces and then station yourself in between them so you can absorb warmth. Set up a campfire 6 to 8 feet from a natural reflector, such as a rock wall, then erect a stone or green log on the other side of the fire. Position yourself in the space between the fire and the wall, and prepare to get toasty. —R.J.

76 BUILD A BRUSH RAFT TO CROSS A RAGING RIVER

You're thinking: "Build a survival raft? When will I ever need to do that?" So consider this: Not long ago, a hiker in New Mexico's Gila National Forest was trapped on the far side of the Gila River after it rose too high for her to wade back. She managed to survive five weeks before being rescued. In fact, crossing raging rivers is a survival situation outdoorsmen often face.

Here is an easy way to build a brush raft. It's designed to keep your gear dry while you swim and push it ahead of you. Though it's buoyant enough to keep you from drowning, it can't support your full weight. You'll need a poncho (or a tarp), which determines its size. Tie a rope to the raft to hold on to while crossing. —K.M.

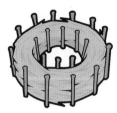

STEP 1 Drive sticks into the ground to outline an inner and outer circle. The diameter should be about half the poncho's width. Weave limbs, saplings, and other wood into a doughnut shape, using the stakes as a guide.

STEP 2 Secure the woven materials with whatever cordage is available— vines, peeled bark, bootlaces, strips from your shirt.

STEP 3 Place the brush raft on top of the poncho and put the hood on the inner side of the doughnut. Tie the neck with the drawstring so it won't let in water.

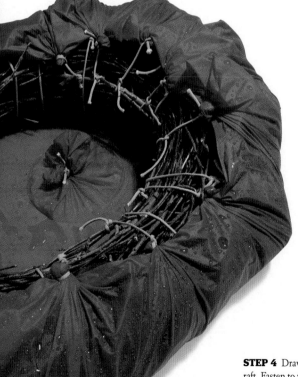

STEP 4 Draw the sides of the poncho up over the raft. Fasten to the brush via grommets or by tying cordage around small stones wrapped in the material.

77 FIND FOOD ABOVE THE TREE LINE

The farther north you go, the lower the tree line. But life—and hence food—exists even where trees do not. Depending on where you are in the world, the fauna and flora will vary, but small animals and birds are probably your best bet. They live among the rocks and low-growing foliage, where you can set snare traps along their preferred routes of travel. In subalpine regions, ruffed grouse (called "dumb chickens" for a reason) are easy to approach and kill. Also use the offal of a previously killed animal as bait to attract birds of prey and four-footed predators, and while they are paying attention to the bait, take them out with a stick or rock. —R.J.

78 TIE A WATER KNOT

You can repair blown webbing or make an emergency harness out of loose webbing with this never-say-die knot, the water knot.

STEP 1 Make an overhand knot in one end of the webbing.

STEP 2 With the second end of your webbing, follow the overhand knot backward through the knot. Make sure this second webbing does not cross over the first. Keep at least 3 inches of tail ends free.

STEP 3 Set the knot with your full weight against the webbing or in the harness. —T.E.N.

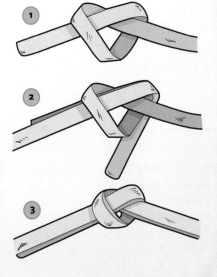

79 REMOVE A LEECH

Leeches are sneaky, waterborne, bloodsucking worms that attach themselves to your skin with suckers (which, conveniently, they have at both ends). The best defense is to cover your body and tuck your pants into your boots. To dislodge a leech, slide your fingernail under a sucker. Work fast, since the leech will try to reattach itself while you're working on the sucker at the opposite end. Clean the wound to prevent infection.—R.J.

80 SURVIVE A LIGHTNING STRIKE

There are lots of snappy sayings to help you remember lightning safety: When the thunder roars, get indoors! If you can see it, flee it! But what do you do when you're caught outdoors with almost nowhere to hide? Try this.

NEAR YOUR VEHICLE OR AN ENCLOSED STRUCTURE Get inside something—your car, a house, a barn. Open structures such as picnic shelters provide little to no protection.

OUT CAMPING Avoid open fields and ridgetops if camping during seasons when thunderstorms are prevalent. Stay away from tall, isolated trees, fence lines, and metal. Move into a lower stand of trees if possible; a tent provides no protection.

IN OPEN COUNTRY Avoid the high ground and points of contact with dissimilar objects, such as water and land, boulders and land, or single trees and land. Head for ditches, gullies, or low ground, and clumps of trees and shrubs of uniform height. Spread out: Group members should be at least 15 feet apart.

ON THE WATER Head inside a boat cabin, which offers a safer environment. Stay off the radio unless it is an emergency. Drop anchor and get as low in the boat as possible. If you're in a canoe on open water, get as low in the canoe as possible and as far as possible from any metal object. If shore only offers rocky crags and tall isolated trees, stay in the boat.

AT THE LAST MOMENT When your hair is standing on end, it's almost too late. Many experts believe that the "Lightning Crunch" provides little to no protection for direct or close strikes, but at this point, some action is better than nothing. Put your feet together and balance on the balls of your feet. Squat low, tuck your head, close your eyes, and cover your ears. —T.E.N.

81 FIND A LOST PERSON

Lose a party member in the backcountry, and you shouldn't sit around until search and rescue arrives. Here's the drill for putting on your own manhunt while waiting for the pros.

PLOT THE POSITION Mark a map with the letters PLS (for "point last seen") at the lost individual's last known position. Draw 3- and 6-mile radius circles around the PLS. Half of all lost persons will be found within the 3-mile circle, and 9 out of 10 within the 6-mile range. If the PLS is within a 10-minute walk, immediately hike there, yelling and whistling every 30 seconds.

CONTAIN THE DAMAGE Make a list of likely high-traffic areas that the lost person might stumble across and send someone to mark the area with notes, daypacks, and directions back to camp.

USE YOUR HEAD Get into the lost person's brain. Think of where he could have lost his way.

ESTABLISH SEARCH TEAMS Make sure searchers have a way to navigate and communicate and then agree on specific times and locations for meeting up again. Send one team to the PLS and send the others to places identified as likely areas.

STOP AT NIGHT If it's not a true emergency, suspend the search after dark.
—T.E.N.

82 SPARK FIRE WITH A KNIFE

Use a high-carbon steel blade or scrounge up an ax head or steel file; stainless steel blades won't work. Find a hunk of hard stone. Besides flint, quartz, quartzite, and chert work well. The trick is to stay away from round rocks; you need one with a ridge sharp enough to peel minuscule slivers of metal from the steel. When they catch fire from friction, that's what causes the spark. Add highly flammable tinder. Start sparking.

STEP 1 Hold the stone with the sharp ridge on a horizontal plane extending from your hand. Depending on where the sparks land, hold a piece of char cloth, tinder fungus, dry grass bundle, or Vaseline-soaked cotton ball under your thumb and on top of the rock, or set the fire-starting material on the ground.

STEP 2 If you're using a fixed-blade knife or ax head, wrap the sharp edge with a piece of leather or cloth. With the back of the blade, strike the stone with a glancing, vertical blow. If the tinder is

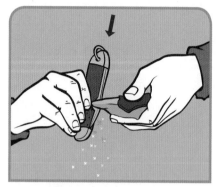

flint and knife blade

flint and file

flint and ax head

on the ground, aim the sparks down toward it.

STEP 3 Gently blow any embers or coals into a flame.

—T.E.N.

83 IMPROVISE A SKEWER HOOK

If you don't have a regular skewer hook, you can make one from a needle-shape sliver of sharpened hardwood or bone. Tie a line to the middle of the skewer, and put a daub of tree sap on the knot to keep it from slipping off. Then turn the skewer parallel with the fishing line and bury it in the bait. When the fish takes the bait, the skewer turns sideways, hooking the fish. And there you have it—fresh fish for supper!—R.J.

84 BREAK BIGGER BRANCHES

No ax, no saw, and here comes the bitter cold. In such a situation, knowing what to do can mean the difference between a cozy bivvy and a frigid one. The trick is to break unwieldy limbs of dead and downed trees into usable 18-inch sections. When you need heartier fuel than what you can render by breaking a few branches across your knee, turn to these useful methods.

FIRE GIRDLE You can use your campfire to help you by digging a small trench radiating outward from the fire, then scraping hot coals into the trench to fill it. Place larger branches across the coals and rotate them. Once they are partially burned through, they will be easy to break.

TREE-CROTCH LEVER Find a sturdy tree crotch about waist high. Insert a dead tree branch into the crotch and push or pull the ends until the wood breaks. This is the quickest way to render dead branches up to 20 feet long into campfire-size chunks.

KNIFE NOTCH Cut a V-notch into one side of a branch, lean it against a tree trunk or place one end on top of a rock, and kick the branch at the notch.

TWO-MAN PUSH-PULL Two men can break a long branch into pieces by centering the branch on a sturdy tree and pushing or pulling against opposite ends. —T.E.N.

85 RID BIG GAME OF HARMFUL BACTERIA

In a long-term survival situation, you'll need to hunt or trap animals for food. Almost all animal life is edible, but there are safety concerns.

BUGS, TINY AND BIG Handling game animals puts you at risk of bacterial diseases such as tularemia. To avoid bites from infected insects, apply insect repellent. When butchering animals, wear long sleeves and pants—and gloves, if possible. And even if you like your steak rare when you're in civilization, cook meat you've hunted until it's well done.

HANTAVIRUS When butchering any animal, don't inhale the dust near its droppings and urine—it could carry this virus, which affects the pulmonary system.

PLAGUE Fleas from infected animals transmit plague to humans. Even after the animal is dead, the fleas will be active, but your gloves, long sleeves, and long pants—you are wearing them, right?—will protect you.

POOP When preparing an animal that you've shot in the gut, clean away matter from the digestive tract. And, as always, cook it thoroughly.—R.J.

86 REMOVE A TICK

Great. In all your wilderness survival fun, you've managed to pick up a hitchhiker. Ticks are nasty little buggers that carry diseases. The longer one stays embedded in its host (that'd be you), the greater the chances are for exposure to the not-too-fun illnesses it may carry. Check often for ticks, especially on your head, armpits, and groin. Also look under clothes in areas like the waistband of your pants.

The best removal method is to grasp the tick near the head and pull straight back. You can use a fancy tick-removal tool if you have one; otherwise, tweezers are your best bet. Avoid squeezing the body of the tick, as that might push tick juice into the wound. Coaxing a tick to back out with a hot needle, match, or petroleum jelly is an old wives' tale. Ticks close their mouths once they've latched on to a host, and unless you pull them off, they only let go when they're done feeding.—R.J.

87 GET WATER FROM A TRANSPIRATION BAG

One of the quickest, easiest, and most effective ways of gathering emergency water in a vegetated environment is to mine the leaves of surrounding trees and bushes. It's a snap, and it can save your life.

Look for a leafy tree in bright sunshine. Place a small rock in a plastic bag, then shimmy the bag over a leafy limb. Be careful not to puncture the bag. Blow the bag up to create smooth surfaces for water condensation. Tie off the bag opening as tightly as possible. Work the rock down into the end of the bag so that one corner of the bag is lower than the ends of the limbs. As sunlight heats the bag and vegetation, evaporated water will condense on the bag's inner surface and drip into the lowest corner. Simply pour it out or insert a length of tubing or a hollow grass reed into the mouth of the bag so you can drain the collected water without removing the bag from the limb. Don't forget to purify water collected in the wild. —T.E.N.

88 TWO ALASKAS

The idea that there are two Alaskas came to me in a cold wave as my canoe was swept into the toppled trees and I was thrown overboard. I caught a glimpse of my pal, Scott Wood, sprinting toward me across an upstream gravel bar, knowing that this was what we had feared the most. Wood disappeared into the brush, running for my life, and then the river sucked me under, and I did not see anything else for what seemed like a very long time.

Every angler dreams of Alaska. My dream was of untouched waters, uncountable salmon and trout, and an unguided route through mountains and tundra. But day after day of portages and hairy paddling had suggested that mine was a trip to the other Alaska, a place that suffers no prettied-up pretense. The other Alaska is not in brochures. It is rarely in dreams. The other Alaska will kill you.

We'd had plenty of postcard moments, for sure: king salmon jetting rooster tails over gravel bars. Tundra hills pocked with snow. Monster rainbows and sockeye salmon heaving for oxygen as we held their sagging bellies. But day after day the four of us had paddled through the other Alaska, scared to death, except when the fishing was good enough to make us forget the fear.

Now the world turned black and cold as the Kipchuk River covered me, my head under water, my arm clamped around a submerged tree, my body pulled horizontal in the hurtling current. Lose my grip and the river would sweep me into a morass of more downed trees and roiling current, so I held on ever tighter as water filled my waders. The river felt like a living thing, attempting to swallow me, inch by inch, and all I could do was hold my breath and hang on.

I can't say how long I hung there, underwater. Twenty seconds, perhaps? Forty?

For long moments I knew I wouldn't make it. I pulled myself along the sunken trunk as the current whipped me back and forth. But the trunk grew larger and larger. It slipped from the grip of my right armpit, and then I held fast to a single branch, groping for the next with my other hand. I don't remember holding my breath. I don't remember the frigid water. I just remember that the thing that was swallowing me had its grip on my shins, then my knees, and then my thighs. For an odd few moments I heard a metallic ringing in my ears. A scene played across my brain: It was the telephone in my kitchen at home, and it was ringing, and Julie was walking through the house looking for the phone, and I suddenly knew that if she answered the call—was the phone on the coffee table? did the kids have it in the playroom?—that the voice on the other end of the line would be apologetic and sorrowful. Then the toe of my right wading boot dragged on something hard, and I stood up in the river, and I could breathe.

Wood crashed through the brush, wild-eyed, as I crawled up the river bank, heaving water. I waved him downstream, then clambered to my feet and started running. Somewhere below was my canoeing partner.

—T. EDWARD NICKENS
Field & Stream, "The Descent," June 2007

89 NAVIGATE BY THE NIGHT SKY

People who are lost in the wilderness have turned their eyes upward for direction since long before man slew his first mammoth. Even today, the moon and stars can provide all the help you need to find your way home.

NORTH BY NORTH STAR

Polaris is the only star in the northern hemisphere that doesn't travel. It always points within 2 degrees of true north, making orientation simple. Locate the pointer stars on the bucket of the Big Dipper in Ursa Major. Observe the spacing between the two stars and then follow their direction five equal spaces to Polaris. You can also fix the position of Polaris, which is not a particularly bright star, using Cassiopeia.

DIRECTIONS BY MOONLIGHT

By noting when the moon rises, it's simple to tell east from west. When the moon rises before midnight, the illuminated side faces west. If it rises after midnight, the illuminated side faces east.

LET THE HUNTER BE YOUR GUIDE

During hunting season in the northern hemisphere, Orion can be found patrolling the southern horizon. This one is easy to spot because Orion rises due east and sets due west and the three horizontal stars that form his belt line up on an east-west line.

SIGHT ON A STAR

You can roughly calculate your direction by noting the path of a star's travel (with the exception of Polaris, all stars rise in the east and set in the west). Face the star of your choice, and drive a stick into the ground. Next back up 10 feet and drive in a second stick so that the two sticks line up pointing toward the star you've chosen. If the star seems to fall after a few minutes of observation, you are facing west; if it rises, you are facing east; if it curves to the right, you are facing south; if it curves to the left, you are facing north. Can't find a stick? Use the open sights on your rifle or the crosshairs of the scope to sight on the star and then track its movement by its deviation from the sights.

—K.M.

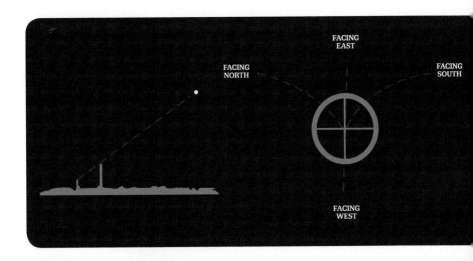

90 SURVIVE IN FAST WATER

Maybe you fell out of your fishing boat, or maybe you slipped while wading the river. Either way, you're suddenly sucked downstream into a long, violent rapid. What do you do?

STEP 1 The safest way to ride a rapid is on your back, with your head pointed upstream, your feet pointing downstream, legs flexed, and toes just above the water's surface. Lift your head to watch ahead. Use your feet to bounce off rocks and logs.

STEP 2 Choking on water will unleash a panic reaction in even the most experienced swimmer. The surest way to avoid a sudden, massive gulp of water is to inhale in the troughs (low points) and exhale or hold your breath at the crests (tops) of the waves.

STEP 3 You will naturally look downstream to avoid obstacles, such as logjams, but don't forget to also scan the shoreline for calmer water, such as an eddy on the downstream side of a rock or river bend.

STEP 4 As the current carries you toward quieter water, paddle with your arms and kick with your legs to steer yourself toward shore. When you get close, roll onto your stomach and swim upstream at a 45-degree angle, which will ferry you to the bank. —K.M.

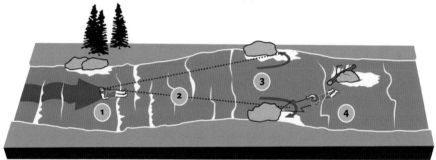

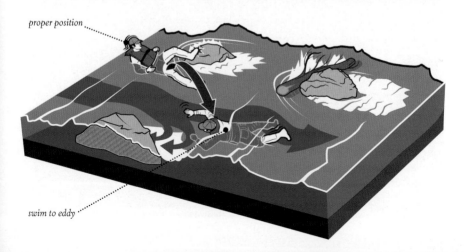

proper position

swim to eddy

91 GET NOTICED BY RESCUERS

Let's face it: The great outdoors isn't all that great when you're stuck in the wilderness and need assistance—and quick. Ideally, you already have key rescue tools (such as fire-starting equipment and both audible and visible signal devices) at your disposal. If all else fails, use these tactics to hasten your rescue.

SCOUT WISELY Make yourself more visible by positioning yourself in a clearing or at a higher elevation. This placement allows you to be both seen and heard from a greater distance.

EMPLOY YOUR GADGETS Try your cell phone or two-way radio, and turn on your personal locator beacon (PLB). Don't leave your phone on to search for a signal, as the battery will drain quickly. Instead, turn it on at intervals as you travel, and cross your fingers.

SIGNAL WITH FIRE Set up three signal fires (widely recognized as a distress signal) and keep an ignition source handy. At any sign that a rescuer might be nearby, get all the fires going. The smoke will attract attention by day, and the flames will draw it by night.

SHINE A LIGHT Use a signal mirror during daylight hours. If you don't have a mirror handy, check your possessions for any metal object that you can work into a shine.

SPELL IT OUT Use color, contrast, and an SOS symbol on the ground to attract the eyes of searchers.

MAKE A MESS Disturb your surroundings to signal that things aren't right by beating down tall grasses, knocking over saplings, removing tree branches, and pushing rocks around.

SEND UP A FLAG Hoist a colored fabric panel to serve as a wind-driven signal flag.—R.J.

92 KEEP MOSQUITOES AT BAY

Mosquitoes are attracted to dark clothing, perspiration, carbon dioxide from your breath, lactic acid produced by exercise, and sweet smells like perfume and deodorant. So don't wear dark clothes, and when you exercise, don't get sweaty or breathe heavily. And don't wear aftershave.

Those things are easier said than done (except for shunning aftershave), but there are lots of ways to avoid mosquito bites. Natural repellents include oils made from cinnamon, cedar, eucalyptus, and several types of flowers. In the wild, where those oils might be unavailable, coat your skin with mud and sit near a smoky fire. Making camp on a windy ridgeline also helps keep mosquitoes away. —R.J.

93 HEAL WITH BUGS

Typically, you want to avoid bugs as much as possible when you're out in the woods (or heck, even in your kitchen for that matter). That is, of course, unless they can be useful to you. Many cultures use the local insects medicinally, and you can too, in a pinch.

WEB BANDAGES A spiderweb can make a sterile bandage for a small cut or abrasion. Find a web and smear it over the injury to prevent infection.

TISSUE THERAPY Maggots are great for removing decayed flesh. Place the insects in a wound and let them feast until only healthy pink tissue remains.

ANT SUTURES Use ants to close a wound. Let them bite both sides of a laceration, then break off their bodies, leaving their heads and mandibles attached.—R.J.

94 BUILD A SNOW CAVE

So you're on a slope and there aren't many shelter options. You're not done for yet—you can burrow your own snow cave and keep warm in freezing conditions.

STEP ONE You need deep snow, preferably on a hillside so you can dig straight in. Begin with a low entrance just large enough for you to crawl inside.

STEP TWO After you've managed to penetrate about 2 feet into the snow, start carving upward to create a dome 4 to 5 feet tall and 6 feet wide.

STEP THREE Against the back wall, shape a sleeping bench 2 feet up from the floor. Poke a small hole in the roof beside the door as an air vent.

STEP FOUR Cover the entrance with a snow block, then heat the interior with a single candle.—R.J.

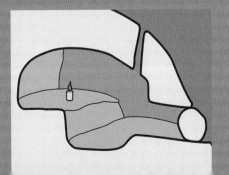

95 FIND WATER IN THE DESERT

The old standby, a solar still, has fallen out of favor. Instead, search for water in the immediate area during the cooler hours of the day. First look in cracks and pockets in rocks and then dig into seep springs in side gullies. Then search for animal trails that converge—they will often lead to water sources. Find a high vantage point and glass for reflections in the desert that could indicate ranch pipelines or small stock ponds in the area. Truly desperate measures include wiping dew off a poncho or car hood. Such efforts may sound crazy, but every half-pint of water can buy you a few hours of lucid thought. —T.E.N.

FIELD & STREAM

In every issue of *Field & Stream* you'll find a lot of stuff: beautiful photography and artwork, adventure stories, wild game recipes, humor, commentary, reviews, and more. That mix is what makes the magazine so great, what's helped it remain relevant since 1895. But at the heart of every issue are the skills. The tips that explain how to land a big trout, the tactics that help you shoot the deer of your life, the lessons that teach you how to survive a cold night outside—those are the stories that readers have come to expect from *Field & Stream*.

You'll find a ton of those skills in this book, but there's not a book big enough to hold them all in one volume. Besides, whether you're new to hunting and fishing or an old pro, there's always more to learn. You can continue to expect *Field & Stream* to teach you those essential skills in every issue. Plus, there's all that other stuff in the magazine, too, which is pretty great. To order a subscription, visit www.fieldandstream.com/subscription.

FIELDANDSTREAM.COM

When *Field & Stream* readers aren't hunting or fishing, they kill hours (and hours) on www.fieldandstream.com. And once you visit the site, you'll understand why. If you enjoy the skills in this book, there's plenty more online—both within our extensive archives of stories from the writers featured here, as well as our network of 50,000-plus experts who can answer all of your questions about the outdoors.

At Fieldandstream.com, you'll get to explore the world's largest online destination for hunters and anglers. Our blogs, written by the leading experts in the outdoors, cover every facet of hunting and fishing and provide constant content that instructs, enlightens, and always entertains. Our collection of adventure videos contains footage that's almost as thrilling to watch as it is to experience for real. And our photo galleries include the best wildlife and outdoor photography you'll find anywhere.

Perhaps best of all is the community you'll find at Fieldandstream.com. It's where you can argue with other readers about the best whitetail cartridge or the perfect venison chili recipe. It's where you can share photos of the fish you catch and the game you shoot. It's where you can enter contests to win guns, gear, and other great prizes. And it's a place where you can spend a lot of time. Which is OK. Just make sure to reserve some hours for the outdoors, too.

THE TOTAL OUTDOORSMAN CHALLENGE

If you enjoyed this book, we encourage you to check out the book it was excerpted from, *The Total Outdoorsman*. This collection of 374 skills covering Camping, Fishing, Hunting, and Survival will make you a true outdoors expert. You'll be ready to take on the world—or at least the wild. Go for it. But you might also consider displaying your newly acquired skills in another arena: the Total Outdoorsman Challenge.

Since 2004, *Field & Stream* has ventured on an annual countrywide search for the nation's best all-around outdoorsman—the person who's equally competent with a rifle, shotgun, bow, rod, and paddle, the person who can do it all. And whoever proves he can do it all walks away with the Total Outdoorsman title, as well as tens of thousands of dollars in cash and prizes.

The Total Outdoorsman Challenge is about more than hunting and fishing though. The event celebrates our belief that the more outdoor skills you have, the more fun you can have in the woods and on the water. It celebrates the friendships that can only happen between sportsmen. Every year thousands of sportsmen compete in the Total Outdoorsman Challenge, and every year many of those competitors meet new hunting and fishing buddies.

So, if you're ready, you should consider testing your skills in the Total Outdoorsman Challenge. (Visit www.totaloutdoorsmanchallenge.com to learn more about the event.) And if you're not sure you're quite ready, you can always read the book again.

INDEX

ACKNOWLEDGMENTS

From the Author, T. Edward Nickens

I would like to thank all of the talented people who made this book possible, including the *Field & Stream* staff editors who guided this project with great care and insight. *Field & Stream* field editors Phil Bourjaily, Keith McCafferty, John Merwin, and David E. Petzal, and editor-at-large Kirk Deeter, provided unmatched expertise. Just good enough is never good enough for them. I wish I could name all the guides, outfitters, and hunting, fishing, and camping companions I've enjoyed over the years. Every trip has been a graduate course in outdoor skills, and much of the knowledge within the covers of this book I've learned at the feet of others. And last, thanks to my longtime field partner, Scott Wood, who has pulled me out of many a bad spot, and whose skillful, detailed approach to hunting and fishing is an inspiration.

From *Field & Stream*'s Editor, Anthony Licata

I would like to thank Weldon Owen publisher Roger Shaw, executive editor Mariah Bear, and art director Iain Morris, who have put together a book filled with skills that have stood the test of time—in a package that should do the same. I'd also like to thank Eric Zinczenko, *Field & Stream* VP and Group Publisher, for championing the Total Outdoorsman concept in all its forms. This great collection of skills would not have been possible without the hard work of the entire *Field & Stream* team, and I'd particularly like to thank Art Director Sean Johnston, Photo Editor Amy Berkley, former Art Director Neil Jamieson, Executive Editor Mike Toth, Managing Editor Jean McKenna, Deputy Editor Jay Cassell, Senior Editor Colin Kearn, and Associate Editor Joe Cermele. I'd also like to thank Sid Evans for his role in creating the Total Outdoorsmen concept. Finally, I'd like to thank my father, Joseph Licata, who first brought me into the fields and streams and showed me what being a total outdoorsman really meant.

CREDITS

CONTRIBUTORS

T. Edward Nickens (T.E.N.) is Editor-at-Large of *Field & Stream* magazine. Known for do-it-yourself wilderness adventures and profiles about people and places where hunting and fishing are the heart and soul of a community, he has chased ptarmigan and char north of the Arctic Circle, antelope in Wyoming, and striped marlin from a kayak in Baja California. He will not turn down any assignment that involves a paddle or a squirrel. Author of the magazine's "Total Outdoorsman" skills features, he also is host, writer, and co-producer for a number of *Field & Stream*'s television and Web shows, among them *The Total Outdoorsman Challenge* and *Heroes of Conservation*. Nickens has been a National Magazine Award finalist, and has won more than 30 writing awards, including three "Best of the Best" top honors awards from the Outdoor Writers Association of America. He lives in Raleigh, North Carolina, within striking distance of mountain trout, saltwater fly fishing, and a beloved 450-acre hunting lease that has been the cause of many a tardy slip for his two school-age children.

Keith McCafferty (K.M.) writes the "Survival" and "Outdoor Skills" columns for *Field & Stream*, and contributes adventure narratives and how-to stories to the magazine and Fieldandstream.com. McCafferty has been nominated for many National Magazine Awards over the years, most recently for his February 2007 cover story, "Survivor." McCafferty's assignments for *Field & Stream* have taken him as far as the jungles of India and as close to home as his backyard. McCafferty lives in Bozeman, Montana, with his wife, Gail. McCafferty loves to fly fish for steelhead in British Columbia and climb the Rockies in pursuit of bull elk.

Rich Johnson (R.J.) is a former Special Forces paratrooper and demolitions expert for the U.S. Army. In his civilian life, he has served as a Coast Guard auxiliary instructor, as well as an EMT and volunteer firefighter, when not enjoying his hobbies of scuba diving, sailing, or backcountry skiing. He specializes in urban survival, emergency preparedness, and primitive living techniques, and once spent a year surviving in the desert wilderness with his wife and small children—who are still talking to him even though part of the project involved living in a cave and eating bugs. He's written extensively on survival topics for *Outdoor Life* magazine and is the author of *Rich Johnson's Guide to Wilderness Survival* and *The Ultimate Survival Manual*.

Additional text by: Robert F. James

"Much of the value of knowing how to survive when you lose all your chips is that the knowledge helps you play a better hand when you're still holding a few decent cards"

—T. Edward Nickens

Please visit our website, **www.garethstevens.com**. For a free color catalog of all our high-quality books, call toll free 1-800-542-2595 or fax 1-877-542-2596.

Library of Congress Cataloging-in-Publication Data

Nickens, T Edward.
Field & stream's guide to outdoor survival / by T. Edward Nickens.
p. cm. — (Field & stream's guide to the outdoors)
Includes index.
ISBN 978-1-4824-2304-4 (library binding)
1. Wilderness survival — Handbooks, manuals, etc. — Juvenile literature.
2. Outdoor life — Handbooks, manuals, etc. — Juvenile literature.
3. Hunting — Juvenile literature. I. Nickens, T Edward. II. Title.
GV191.62 N53 2015
796.5 —d23

Published in 2015 by
Gareth Stevens Publishing
111 East 14th Street, Suite 349
New York, NY 10003

© 2015 Weldon Owen Publishing

President, CEO: Terry Newell
VP, Publisher: Roger Shaw
Executive Editor: Mariah Bear
Creative Director: Kelly Booth
Art Director: William van Roden

Designer: Meghan Hildebrand
Cover Design: William Mack
Illustration Coordinator: Conor Buckley
Production Director: Chris Hemesath
Production Manager: Michelle Duggan

Printed in the United States of America
CPSIA compliance information: Batch CW15GS: For further information contact Gareth Stevens, New York, New York at 1-800-542-2595.

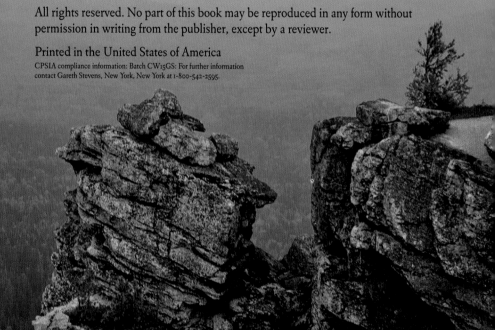